This Is a Leaf

A lotus leaf

This Is a Leaf

ROSS E. HUTCHINS

Photographs by the author

DODD, MEAD & COMPANY

NEW YORK

Contents

Introduction

This is the story of leaves, without which we could not live. Leaves flutter upon the twigs of tall jungle trees and hide themselves among the rocks of the Arctic tundra. They clothe the prairies with carpets of green and form a canopy that shades the forest from the hot sun of summer. Leaves plus water make the difference between the desert and the sylvan glade.

On the pages that follow you will read about leaves that guide the traveler like magnetic compasses, of leaves that sleep, and of leaves that capture and eat animals. You will also learn how leaves manufacture the world's food as well as its most potent poisons and drugs. Here, too, is told the story of autumn leaves and how Nature paints the forests with red and gold. You will also learn how the leaves of the ancient past became the leaves of today.

This, then, is the story of Nature's most remarkable invention —the green leaf.

—R. E. H.

Magnolia leaves in the rain. Green leaves, with the aid of sunlight plus water and minerals absorbed from the soil, manufacture starches and sugars. Leaves furnish shade from the sun, alter the world's climates, and provide hundreds of things we need.

CHAPTER 1

Leaves in Your Life

Leaves are found everywhere. They festoon the twigs of dwarf willows along Arctic seas and clothe the great trees of tropical jungles with a green canopy. The leaves of seaside morning-glories add their touch of green to ocean beaches, and upon most of our loftiest mountain tops you will find leafy plants nestled among the protective rocks. They push up through the margins of glacial snows and emerge from cracks in the hot pavements of our city streets.

Today perhaps you walked through a forest or a city park. If it is winter, the trees were bare with gaunt limbs stretching up to the sky. You saw no leaves, but they were there just the same. Each bud contained a tiny embryo leaf that will unfold with the coming of spring. Summer, of course, is the time of leaves, and the yearly cycle of the leaves is one of the miracles of Nature. When the leaves of spring unfold, they are soft and tender. Each one is perfect. But as the season progresses, their textures become rough and their forms ragged from winds and the feeding of a thousand different kinds of insects. With the arrival of autumn many leaves change to gold or scarlet and then drop from the trees upon which they grew. They usually live but a season and then drop to the earth and turn to leaf mold and humus. During the following winter the moisture, aided by fungi and molds, converts the tissues of the fallen leaves back again into

The spear-like leaves of the century plant are thick and filled with stored water. The leaves also manufacture food like any other green leaf.

nourishment for the growing leaves of another year. Year after year, season after season, that is the cycle of the leaves.

Leaves come in endless variety. Probably there is no shape the human mind can conceive that is not found in some leaf. Most people can identify common plants and trees by their leaves. That is because each plant or tree has a characteristic type of leaf. Most of us do this unconsciously, without stopping to think about it. We recognize an oak because it has oak leaves, and an elm because it is covered with elm leaves. Of course, we also use other characteristics, such as general shape and bark texture, but we rely a great deal upon leaves.

Leaves are a little like fingerprints—no two leaves, even from the same tree or plant, are ever just exactly alike. If we compare them under a microscope, we find small differences in the branching of the veins and in the arrangements of the hairs. Yet, each leaf is characteristic of the plant or tree upon which it grows. We can identify a person by means of his fingerprints, and we can almost always identify a tree or plant by its leaves. Leaves are the trademarks of the trees.

The primary purpose of leaves is the manufacture of food and

10

other things the growing plant needs, but Nature has often modified or changed leaves so that they serve the plant in other ways. The tendrils of pea vines are, in truth, merely specialized leaves. The pea plant uses these twining tendrils to anchor itself to trellises or fences. Some leaves, such as those of the century plant, are very thick and are used for the storage of water. It may surprise you to learn that the colorful petals of flowers are really leaves which Nature has dressed up in bright colors that attract insects which help to bring about pollination. Things in nature are not always what they seem. You have no doubt noticed the green scale-like structures just beneath the petals of many flowers. Botanists call these *bracts*. In the case of dogwood, however, the actual flowers are very small, and the large white "petals" are really bracts. Bracts in turn are actually modified leaves.

One of the most unusual uses to which plants put their leaves is that of capturing insect prey. These are truly amazing plants. There are a number of different kinds, and they thrive in many

The pitcher plant adds to its food supply by "eating" insects. This kind has bright red veins in its hollow leaves. Insects are attracted to their doom inside the leaf-traps.

places in the world. Some of these "believe-it-or-not" plants have leaves that are hollow and shaped like pitchers—the pitcher plants. Into these leaf-traps many insects are lured to their dooms. You have no doubt heard of, or perhaps seen, the Venus flytrap. In this case the leaf is hinged at the center and has teeth along its margins in such a way that it can snap shut upon any insect foolish enough to stray upon it. The leaves of these plants are green, and, in addition to capturing and digesting prey, they manufacture starchy foods like any other green leaf.

While the primary work of green leaves is the manufacturing of starches and other foods with the aid of sunlight, this work, in some cases, is carried on by other parts of a plant. In many members of the cactus family, for example, the work of food manufacture is carried on by the fleshy stems while the leaves themselves have been changed into protective spines and thorns. Nature is very clever in using what she has to do different kinds of work.

If you have ever been to southern Florida or to almost any other tropical land, you have probably seen *Bromeliads* or "air plants" growing high in trees. Botanically, the air plants belong to the pineapple family, but they have a most unusual method of storing water. The leaves arise in a *basal whorl,* and rain water collects at the bases of the leaves. These plants cannot obtain their moisture from the soil so Nature has fitted the leaf blades together in such a way that each plant may hold a pint or more of rain water. There are a number of other kinds of plants, especially in the Tropics, whose leaves serve as water tanks. In one of these, certain tree frogs lay their eggs in the "leaf ponds" and their tadpoles develop there, high above the ground.

The leaves of plants and trees are always busy manufacturing food whenever the sun is shining. All animal life is dependent upon the foods manufactured by plants and stored in their roots, tubers, and stems. But leaves help us in other ways, too. The roots of plants absorb moisture from the soil, and this moisture

Air plants growing upon trees in tropical forests have the bases of their leaves formed into a "tank" for catching and storing water.

passes up the stems and into the leaves. Here some of it is used by the leaves, but a lot of it is "breathed" out through leaf pores called *stomates*. This moisture or water passes out of the leaves in the form of vapor. You can prove this to yourself by covering any small plant with an inverted drinking glass. Within a few minutes the inside of the glass becomes clouded with droplets of water. This water passed out of the leaf as vapor and condensed on the cool inner surface of the glass. Have you ever

13

Here are shown the exact shapes of thirty-one common tree and shrub leaves. How many of them can you identify? Key to correct answers is on page 118.

entered a greenhouse on a cool day? The air feels very humid, and if you wear glasses they immediately become so clouded with moisture that you cannot see for a minute or so until your glasses become warmed up. All of this adds up to the fact that leaves, by their moisture emission, can change a climate, whether it is inside a greenhouse or in a great forest covering a thousand square miles. In a dense forest the leaves form an almost unbroken canopy high above your head. Botanists have found that in such a forest only about one hundredth of the sunshine that falls upon the tree tops actually penetrates down to reach the forest floor. The rest is absorbed by the numerous tiers of leaves. That is why a deep forest is always cool. But because each leaf is breathing out moisture, the forest is both cool and humid and forms a climate where mosses and ferns thrive.

During the hot part of the day the temperature of a forest is warmest at the tops of the trees and here many heat-loving spiders and insects go. With the coming of night these creatures move downward as the upper story of the forest cools.

If you have ever been in a dense forest during a rain you probably found that you did not get as wet as if you had been out in the open. Scientists have found that less than half of the rain falling upon a forest in summer actually reaches the ground. The raindrops that fall upon the leafy forest canopy are partly absorbed by the leaves and partly evaporated into the air. This moisture-laden air may blow away and thus the climate of the entire region may be changed. On a warm summer day more than 2,500 gallons of water may be "breathed" out of the leaves in an acre of forest. This is equal to fifty 50-gallon drums of water!

Plants and their leaves serve us in endless ways. The next time you are in a supermarket, look about you. Stacked attractively on the shelves are foods of great variety. Some of the foods were produced near your home, but many others were grown in far lands: Africa, South America and India. There are spices from the Far Eastern islands and frozen fishes from distant rivers and seas. There are olives from Spain and bananas from Honduras. These foods all have one thing in common; they are all products of green plants and their leaves. Even the meats and fishes are the end result of leaf activity, for "all flesh is grass." Even the paper and cardboard containers, and the wooden shelves upon which they are stacked, are products of the busy leaves.

Some foods are packed in metal cans, but amazingly, leaves may have had a hand in locating the metal-bearing ores from which came the tin and iron out of which the cans were constructed. Many deposits of ores have been located by studying the plant life of various regions. The presence of tin is often associated with heather, and iron deposits may often be detected by the abundant growth of certain grasses. Many countries, including Russia, are now taking advantage of this fact in their search for metal-bearing ores. Sometimes this search for ores is done by flying over mountainous regions and studying the coloration of the vegetation. In other instances the study is carried on from the ground. In any case, it has been found that when nickel, copper, cobalt, chromium, zinc or manganese is present in the soil in excessive amounts the leaves of plants tend to turn yellow. When aluminum is abundant, leaves are often scorched and mottled. Boron causes foliage to be stunted and darker than normal. The presence of too much cobalt in soil causes dead-white patches to appear in leaves. These are the clues modern geologists are using in their search for valuable ore deposits.

Plants have even made their contribution to the Atomic Age. The presence of uranium may be detected by the presence of strangely shaped fruits and stalked leaf rosettes. Some plants seem to grow more abundantly in areas where uranium occurs. *Astragalus* or vetch plants have been used as clues to locating uranium in Colorado.

16

No matter what we do or where we live, we are still dependent upon green leaves. When men at last realize their dreams of space travel, they will still have to depend upon green plants to feed them. Journeys across the limitless reaches of space will take months, perhaps even years. Space travelers cannot carry enough food to last that length of time, so they will probably have to depend upon foods produced in tanks containing certain kinds of green plants. Wherever spacemen go their space ships will be bathed in sunshine, for the most part, and the plants they carry with them in greenhouse tanks will produce the food they must have to live. Thus we see that even in the depths of space, men will still be dependent upon the green of leaves just as they are upon Earth. To exist for long periods in space, men must take a bit of the green world with them.

In this laboratory scientists are studying microscopic green plants that may be used to feed space travelers.

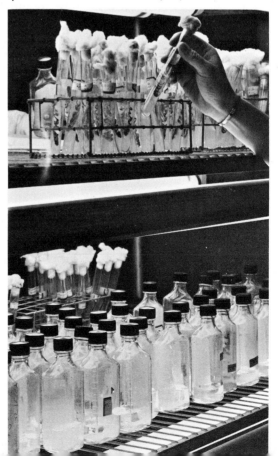

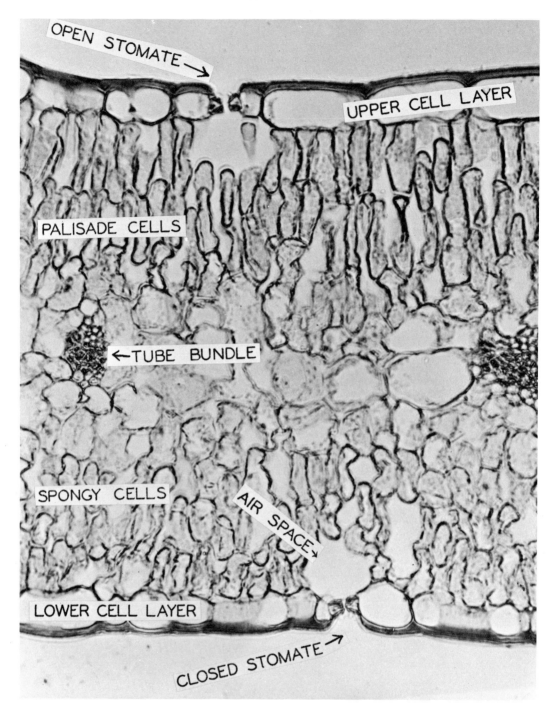

OPEN STOMATE →

UPPER CELL LAYER

PALISADE CELLS

←TUBE BUNDLE

SPONGY CELLS

AIR SPACE →

LOWER CELL LAYER

CLOSED STOMATE →

This is how a thin slice of a leaf looks under a microscope. It is greatly enlarged; the thickness of the leaf from top to bottom is hardly thicker than this paper. The various parts of the leaf's inner structure are labeled.

CHAPTER 2

Leaves at Work

*I*f you pick a leaf off a plant and examine it, it may seem that there is nothing much of interest about it. It has a stem or *petiole* (pronounced pet-e-ol), a main mid-rib, and a network of veins. It is green and may be any one of a thousand different shapes. No two leaves are ever exactly alike. And then, too, leaves from older plants have a finer network of veins than leaves from younger plants. Some leaves are as thick as cardboard while others are as thin as the paper upon which these words are printed.

In order to discover how fascinating leaves can be, you should examine them at very high magnification under a microscope. A hand lens is useful, but it is really not powerful enough to show all the interesting details. Let us first look at the upper side of any ordinary leaf through a microscope. What do we see? Most obvious is the fine network of veins extending to every part. In a blade of grass or a lily leaf these veins run parallel, but in most other plants they form a network. Perhaps the leaf is clothed with hairs or hair-like glands. Some of these glandular hairs, as in the case of the geranium, are knobbed at the tip, but others are many-branched as in the case of the mullein. These plant hairs can be examined easily with a hand lens. Some glandular hairs secrete a sticky substance, and others, like those on the nettle leaf, are filled with a very irritating poison.

The stomates or breathing pores on an iris leaf look like this under a microscope. Each stomate is made up of two sausage-shaped cells with a gap between them. These stomates usually open during the day while the leaf-factory is working and close at night.

If your bare arm is brushed against a nettle leaf, there is an intense itching sensation. This is the plant's method of protecting itself.

In general, both surfaces of a leaf look about the same, but if you have a powerful enough microscope you may be able to see the breathing pores or *stomates*. These are especially abundant on the lower surface. They are best observed by carefully stripping off a tiny bit of the tissue from the lower side and examining it under a microscope. Each of these stomates consists of two kidney-shaped cells placed side by side in such a way that there is a small space between them. These are called *guard cells,* and it is through the gap between them that air enters the inner spaces of the leaf. It is through these stomates, also, that water escapes into the outside air in the form of water vapor. Botanists call this *transpiration.*

The undersides of most plant leaves contain an enormous number of stomates. Each square inch of an apple leaf may have a quarter of a million! In many plants they also occur on the upper surface of the leaves, but in lesser numbers.

These stomates open in the morning and close at night. The manner in which they do so is quite remarkable. When the leaf becomes full of moisture the guard cells absorb water and tend to bend outward. This is because their inner margins are thicker and cannot stretch as the cell expands. This bending action causes a gap to appear between the two guard cells. The stomate is now open and will remain so until night or until too much moisture is lost. Then the guard cells bend back together and close the gap. The stomates work almost automatically, opening and closing to admit or exclude water and air. Light, acting through the chemical processes within the leaf, also affects the opening and closing. This accounts for the fact that they open during the daytime while the leaf-factory is working and close at night when the leaf-factory is shut down. A glance at the accompanying photographs of the two model stomates will help you to understand how they work.

These two models show how leaf stomates, or guard cells, open and close. On the left is a closed stomate; on the right is an open cell. When water in the leaf is absorbed into the stomate cells, they bend outward leaving a gap between. Water vapor may then escape and air may enter the leaf through the open stomate.

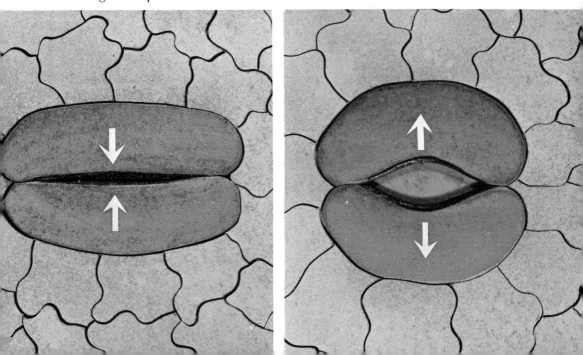

The water that passes out of a plant's stomates is often in very great quantities. Botanists agree that a small amount of water also escapes from the plant in other ways, but at least 90 per cent is lost through the stomates. It has been found that a corn plant transpires about 50 gallons of water during its growth. At this rate, an acre of corn would evaporate nearly 2,000 gallons during the summer. The production of water within a plant is really part of its growth and manufacturing processes. It is estimated that in order to produce a pound of wood, a tree gives off from 200 to 500 pounds of water, and 500 pounds of water are used to grow one pound of hay! It is easy to see that water plays an important part in the lives of plants.

You have probably noticed the gem-like drops of water gleaming in the morning sun at the tips of grass blades and along the leaf margins of other plants. Perhaps you thought this was dew. It isn't. It is another way in which plants lose water. Dew forms as droplets scattered over the surfaces of plants and is the result of condensation from moist night air. The shining droplets at grass tips and leaf margins result when more water arrives from the roots than is needed by the leaves. This water escapes from the leaves through special pores called *water stomates*. Unlike the other stomates, they remain open both day and night, and the escape of excess water in this way is called *guttation*. Water escapes through ordinary stomates in the form of vapor, but that leaving the leaves through the water stomates is in liquid form.

We have now examined both upper and lower surfaces of a leaf. Let us next explore the interior and see what we find. Just below the layer of cells that makes up the upper leaf surface there is a zone of long cells stacked together side by side on end like sardines in a can. There may be several tiers of these cells, each cell filled with the living fluid called *protoplasm*. In these cells there are also many small green "grains." These latter are the *chlorophyll* bodies, and their function is the production of

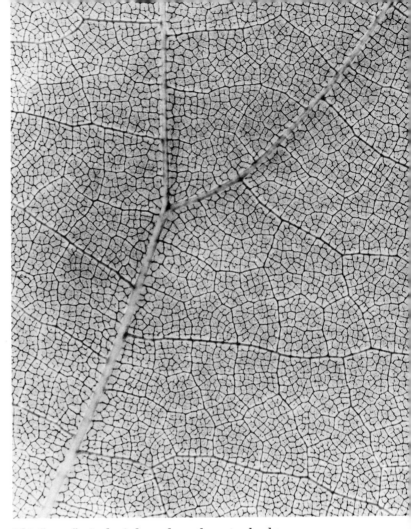

This "x-ray" of a leaf shows how the veins lead to every part. Inside each vein are ducts that carry water to the cells and manufactured food to other parts of the plant.

starch with the aid of sunlight. This zone of cells is called the *palisade* layer because of its resemblance to a palisade which is built by setting tall posts side by side. Just below this region is a zone filled with cells arranged in a sponge-like manner with many spaces between them. These spaces are connected to the outer surfaces of the leaf by the breathing pores or stomates described above.

The other main points of interest in leaf structures are the veins or tubes that extend into all its parts. This system of tubes

This cross-section of the leaf stem or petiole of the water lotus shows the large air passages that lead down from the leaves to the submerged root or tuber and supply it with air.

forms a network within the leaf and also extends down the stem and into the roots. These veins carry water and dissolved chemicals up from the soil, and manufactured foods back down to nourish the various parts of the growing plant.

A plant leaf has often been called a factory, and this is certainly an apt comparison when one realizes that all of the food consumed by animals is manufactured by plants and their leaves. Someone once said, "Green plants stand between the

24

animal world and starvation." It has been estimated that the green plants of the world manufacture about 300 billion tons of sugar each year!

The general structure of a leaf is relatively simple, but just how such a simple thing is able to manufacture sugars, starches and many other things out of water, air and mineral elements has puzzled scientists for centuries. If you doubt that a plant can do this, you could make a rather simple experiment to find out for yourself. It is an experiment performed nearly 500 years ago by Jan Baptista van Helmont in Belgium. He placed 200 pounds of dry soil in a container and planted a willow shoot weighing 5 pounds in it. For five years van Helmont carefully watered the willow. It grew rapidly. At the end of the five years he weighed the tree again and found that it then weighed 164 pounds. He dried the soil and found that it lacked only 2 ounces of weighing 200 pounds. Thus, nearly 159 pounds had been gained from somewhere! But from where? Van Helmont did not know, and several hundred years passed before scientists

If scientists are ever able to build a factory to manufacture sugar with the aid of sunlight, it might look something like this model. A study of the model will help you to understand how green chlorophyll is able to manufacture sugar from water and carbon dioxide gas. The sun furnishes the power.

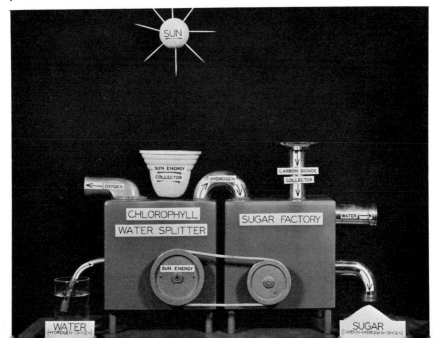

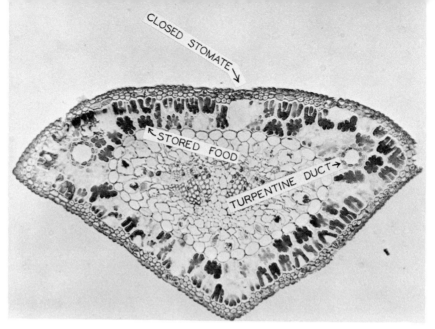

A greatly enlarged cross-section of a pine needle. Note the turpentine ducts and the dark cells filled with stored food.

discovered that plants actually manufacture their own food by the strange process called *photosynthesis*, which means to "put together with light." Chemists now know a great deal about this remarkable ability of green plants to create food materials, but they still do not know exactly how plants do it, and it has never yet been done in the laboratory. Scientists have split the atom and sent rockets rushing into outer space, but they still cannot duplicate the work of green leaves.

How much do scientists really know about *photosynthesis?* In laboratories scattered all over the world chemists are making studies, and little by little they are learning the answers. The chemical processes involved are very complex, but in a brief and simple way, here is how plants are able to form sugars from water and air with the aid of green chlorophyll. Of course, a leaf not only manufactures sugars and starches, but a host of other things, from such poisonous substances as strychnine to sweet smelling oils such as peppermint oil. At present we are concerned only with sugar manufacture.

The air that surrounds the earth is composed of various gases, but the most important ones are oxygen, carbon dioxide and nitrogen. The first two are the ones involved in sugar manufacture by plants. About 20 per cent of ordinary air is oxygen while only about 4 per cent is carbon dioxide. Actually, this latter gas is a compound created by burning fires and by the life processes of animals. The other basic raw material required by plants is water, and this, too, is a compound, formed by the union of gaseous hydrogen and oxygen. Plants obtain water chiefly through their roots, from which it is "pumped" upward through the stems and into the leaves. Here, in the presence of green chlorophyll, water is split into hydrogen and oxygen. The energy of the sun furnishes the power to do this. The gaseous oxygen passes out of the leaf and into the air. At the same time, carbon dioxide gas is entering the leaf through the stomates or breathing pores. Now, by some remarkable chemistry not yet fully understood, the hydrogen gas left over from the splitting of water is combined with the carbon dioxide. The sun also furnishes the energy for this step in the manufacturing process. The result is sugar, a compound containing carbon, hydrogen and oxygen. (If you burn a small amount of sugar, it turns black. This is because the hydrogen and oxygen are driven off, leaving almost pure carbon which is the same thing as soot.)

The above steps in the production of sugar by a leaf may sound quite simple, but actually, the details are but little understood by scientists.

But the importance of food manufacture by plants is well known. These mysterious processes within leaves sustain all life, either directly or indirectly. There is the case of the strange flatworm that takes direct advantage of a plant's ability to produce food. This remarkable creature fills itself with green algae cells that occur on the sea beaches where it lives. The flatworm then stops feeding, and during the rest of its life is nourished by the food so conveniently manufactured by the chlorophyll-bearing algae within its transparent body.

27

The coconut is probably the world's most useful tree. People of tropical climates depend upon it for many of their needs. Houses are thatched with its enormous leaves, the meat of the large nut is nutritious, and the "milk" is a refreshing drink. The trunk furnishes logs for building, and even the fiber surrounding the nut is useful.

CHAPTER 3

The Things They Make

Down the ages men have always been interested in plants and their leaves, but this interest has usually been a selfish one. The plants they studied were usually those that had food value or some supposed medicinal property. The first books about plants were called *herbals,* and these dealt with plants used in curing human ailments. Many of the old beliefs regarding plants seem very foolish to us today. It was once believed that in order to cure a disease one should eat a plant or a portion of a plant that resembled the part of the body affected. If the brain was diseased, ground nutmeg was often prescribed because a nutmeg resembles the brain in appearance. For a disease of the eye, a plant or a root resembling the eye was used. In Europe the mandrake plant was believed to be of great medicinal value because it vaguely resembled a man. It was also believed that when pulled up, a mandrake plant gave a loud shriek.

We know now, of course, that in most instances the plants and leaves that were ground up and prescribed by "herb doctors" were of little or no value. Sometimes, perhaps, they were even harmful to the unfortunate patients.

It is an interesting fact, however, that many common plants get their names from the medical and other uses to which they were put. The nightshade family, for example, which contains many plants very useful to us as foods—peppers, Irish potato,

Plants of the nightshade family manufacture a large number of products useful to us, including peppers of various kinds, Irish potatoes, the drug belladonna, tomatoes, eggplants, and tobacco. Strangely, this family also contains several poisonous plants, as well as petunias.

The leaves of various kinds of mints contain aromatic substances called essential oils. From them we get the seasonings thyme, marjoram, and sage, as well as oil of peppermint, bergamot oil, and catnip. Mint oils are used as flavoring in candy and chewing gum.

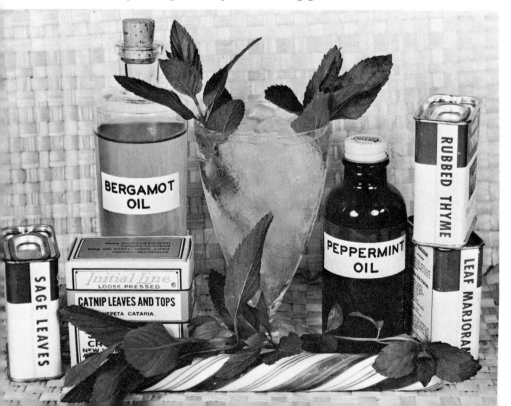

tomato, eggplant and tobacco—is named for the deadly nightshade plant or *belladonna*. An extract of this plant contains the drug called *belladonna* which was once used as eyedrops by fashionable ladies to make the pupils of their eyes large and "mysterious." Belladonna literally means "beautiful." The drug is still used in medicine today. Another plant that received its name as a result of its original use in medicine is the common Joe-Pye weed. Joe Pye was an Indian herb doctor during colonial days. He administered the plant for many ailments.

A close relative of belladonna is the jimson weed, a common plant often found growing in vacant lots. It has an interesting history. In the year 1607 when spring finally came for the Virginia colonists at Jamestown, they were happy to see green leaves again. All winter they had starved, and when they saw tender, green plants pushing up out of the earth they gathered the leaves for "greens." Unfortunately, these "greens" were poisonous members of the nightshade family, and the poisonous drug they contained made the colonists very ill, and several of them died. This tragic incident gave the plant its name, Jamestown-weed, which has been changed with time to "jimson weed."

Plants and their leaves produce an enormous number of drugs, many of which are still sold by druggists and prescribed by doctors. For instance, the cinchona tree produces quinine, long used for the treatment of malaria. From foxglove is obtained digitalis, a powerful heart stimulant. Many common laxatives are still obtained from plants, and such narcotic, or pain-easing drugs, as cocaine, morphine and opium are products of plants and their busy leaves.

Like the jimson weed just mentioned, many plants and their leaves contain very poisonous materials, some of which we have found to be useful. A number of our most effective insecticides are extracted from plants. These include *nicotine* obtained from the tobacco plant, and *pyrethrum* obtained from one variety of chrysanthemum. In several places in the Tropics there grow poisonous plants from which *strychnine* is obtained, a poison used in exterminating harmful rats or coyotes. The Mexican jumping bean plant, a close relative of the strychnine plant, is an unusual shrub which produces the amusing jumping beans often seen in novelty shops, but it also contains a poisonous sap that was once used by the Mexican Indians for poisoning arrows.

There are many common plants that may cause poisoning if the leaves are eaten. Why Nature has caused these leaves to produce these poisons we can only guess. Perhaps their presence helps to protect the plant from leaf-eating insects and other animals. One should always refrain from eating or chewing a leaf, especially from an unknown plant. Even common plants may be poisonous. This includes the leaves of the English ivy, yellow jessamine, oleander and many others.

Besides drugs and poisons of various kinds, leaves also produce *essential oils*. These are not true oils, but they do appear oily and most of them have very pungent odors. These "oils" are often extracted from the plants and used in various ways. In some cases they are extracted from the leaves and in other cases from the flowers, roots or even from bark. Have you ever crushed a mint leaf between your fingers? The pleasing smell came from the presence of oil of mint. Other essential oils are extracted from jasmine, carnation, and rose and used in perfumes. Other plant and leaf "oils" are oil of camphor, oil of citronella, and even oil of turpentine, the latter being obtained from pine. Perhaps the most pleasant smelling and tasting of these essential "oils" are those present in the leaves of various plants of the mint family. These are used to flavor candy and chewing gum.

Plants of the spurge family produce true oils used in both industry and medicine. From the croton plant comes croton oil, a powerful cathartic, while the castor bean plant produces castor oil. The latter plant also produces a poisonous drug which

Among the most useful products of plants and their leaves is cotton, which is made into garments of many kinds and used in numerous other ways.

must be separated from castor oil before it is used as medicine. Castor oil is also an excellent lubricant for certain types of machinery. The tung tree, grown in the southeastern United States, is the source of tung oil much used in paints and varnishes. The spurge family also contains the rubber tree and such common flowering plants as poinsettia and snow-on-the-mountain. The leaves of many of these spurge plants are poisonous.

We are dependent upon plants and leaves for many other things we use. Plants furnish us with most of our clothing in the

The common carrot has some rather strange relatives, among them celery, the assafoetida *plant, caraway, parsley, and flowers such as Queen Anne's lace.*

form of cotton and linen. From cotton plants in our Southland comes the raw cotton which is spun into an endless variety of garments, and from flax comes the fiber which is transformed into linen cloth. The cotton plant, you may be surprised to know, belongs to the hollyhock family.

Other things produced by plants include gums, resins, dyes, and waxes. Some of these may not be obtained directly from leaves, but leaves manufactured the basic substances from which they came. We can also say that the wood present in all trees was manufactured by the leaves. Thus, the very houses we live in are largely products of tree leaves. Actually, this book you are now reading was produced by leaves also, since the materials for it originally came from trees and plant products.

Like any other factory, the leaf factories of plants must have storage depots for the things they produce. Some plants store their food supplies in roots, stems, fruits or nuts, and a large portion of the food we eat comes from this stored plant food. Potatoes, for example, are merely underground storage places where the potato plant hides its supply of nourishment. This same thing is true of radishes, carrots, and turnips. Beets are biennial or two-year plants that store up food in their underground roots one summer and produce flowers and seeds the next. Usually, however, we harvest the beets before they have a chance to bloom. Other plants store their foods in the seeds they produce. This food is for the benefit of the young plants of the next generation that will eventually grow out of each seed— provided it is not eaten by some animal or man first. Examples are corn, nuts of all kinds, wheat, oats and the coconut. In a few cases, such as rhubarb and asparagus, we eat the stems of plants for the nourishment stored there, but in other instances we eat the leaves themselves. Examples of the latter are spinach, turnip greens, lettuce and cabbage.

There are many different families of plants, but strangely enough, most of the useful plants belong to just a few families. We have already seen that the nightshade and spurge families boast of many prominent and valuable members. The rose family, too, contributes freely to our larder, since apples, pears, raspberries, apricots and plums are all included in it. Some of our most common and useful plants are all members of the mustard family. To this group belong many food-producing plants such as rutabaga, turnip, lettuce, cabbage, spinach, radish, and watercress. And the grasses make up another ex-

The plant world contains many surprises. Shown here are leaves of the poison ivy, and a handful of cashew nuts. The plant that produced the delicious nuts is closely related to poison ivy.

tremely useful plant family. To this ancient and venerable line belong the plants that feed the world—wheat, oats, corn, barley, and rice. Without them the people of the world would probably starve.

In examining plant families one finds some strange bedfellows. Botanists often classify plants in ways that do not seem very logical at first glance, yet when we study the details of their flowers and other structures it becomes clear why certain plants are considered to be related. For example, a sunflower and a daisy have similar types of blooms, and both belong to the daisy family. If you see these two plants without their blooms, however, the similarity is not so apparent. We have already noted some seemingly odd plant relationships. One would not think of apples or pears as being relatives of the rose, but they are really "sisters under the skin." The carrot family, too, has some surprising relatives. Celery and parsley seem likely cousins, but poison-hemlock and the plant that produces ill-smelling *asafoetida* are also kin to the common carrot. The cinchona tree which produces quinine, a drug long used to combat malaria, belongs to the same plant family as the coffee tree from which we obtain coffee. Surprisingly, the gardenia is also a member of this family, and the "bean" from which we obtain vanilla for flavoring is actually an orchid! You may find it hard to believe, but the plants that produce both pistachio and cashew nuts are first cousins to ordinary poison ivy. And did you know that garlic and onion plants are really lilies?

Whatever the particular plant family may be, the products manufactured by plants and their leaves are highly important to us. There are hundreds of plant products without which our daily lives would be much less enjoyable. These items, as well as our abundance of foods of all kinds, are, of course, a result of the industry of the world's plant life.

CHAPTER 4

Leaves in the Sun

*L*eaves come in assorted sizes and in endless shapes. They vary in size from the 50-foot leaf fronds of certain tropical palms to the tiny floating leaves of pond duckweeds. Their shapes vary from those resembling stars, diamonds, discs and ovals to slender blades. Some, such as those of the Mexican breadfruit, contain large holes. Leaves, such as those of the maples, are very thin, while others, like those of the century plant, are very thick and are also used for water and food storage. One of the most remarkable leaves in the world is that of the royal water lily (*Victoria regia*), found in the backwaters of the Amazon River. Its circular leaves are nearly ten feet in diameter with up-turned edges two inches high.

Actually, a leaf is merely a flattened portion of the stem that Nature has modified to serve a special purpose: the manufacture of foods and other things needed by the living plant. In general, leaves are temporary structures. They grow and expand in spring and die and fall to the ground at the end of the growing season. Some leaves, however, last for several years. The slender leaves of the pine, for example, remain on the tree for two or three years. The same is true of magnolia leaves. In the Tropics leaves tend to remain on trees longer than those in temperate climates. This is probably because in the warm lands growth goes on continually with no severe winter season which kills most tender foliage.

If you examine a leaf, you will find that it has two main parts, the *blade* or expanded portion, and the *petiole* or leaf stem. Sometimes the petiole is absent, the leaf arising directly from the twig. At the bases of the petioles in many plants are found additional leaf-like structures called *stipules* (pronounced stip-yuls). These are usually considered to be parts of the leaf, and in many cases are quite large and carry on a considerable amount of photosynthesis. Examples of leaves with large stipules are the Japanese quince and the garden pea. There are many others. There are a number of plants in which the stipules have been changed into spines. The sharp spines of cactus plants, on the other hand, are actually greatly modified leaves, the work of food manufacture being carried on by the fleshy, green stems. Thus, the cactus plant has no real leaves at all. The leaves of many different kinds of plants have been adapted to other uses besides food-making. The climbing tendrils of pea plants are, in truth, modified leaves. The leaf petioles of the clematis vine are used to curl about other plants and twigs for support, and the twining tendrils of smilax are actually outgrowths of the leaf petioles.

Botanists classify leaves by types. A *simple* leaf is one in which the blade is all in one piece, as in the case of the cotton-wood or apple. A large number of plants have their leaves divided into several small *leaflets*. There are many examples of this, including ash, hickory, beans, roses, ferns and palms. Such a leaf is said to be *compound*. These compound leaves, in turn, are of several types. In the case of rose, hickory, sumac and ash, the leaflets are placed opposite each other along the central leaf stem. Some compound leaves, by contrast, have the leaflets all arising from one point, as in the case of Virginia creeper and buckeye. Such leaves are said to be *palmately compound* because of their resemblance to the palm of the hand.

If you will observe the leaves of a number of different plants and trees, you will soon realize that they are arranged upon the

LEAF

TENDRILS

STIPULES

PETIOLE

STEM

Leaves come in many forms and shapes. Here is the double leaf of the sweetpea and its tendrils, which are actually leaves that have been changed into organs to help support the plant. The leaf stems or petioles *are winged, and at the bases of many leaves are leaf-like structures called* stipules, *almost as large as the true leaves.*

shoots or twigs in several different ways. Some plants have their leaves placed alternately on opposite sides of the twigs, as do birch, oaks, elms and poplar. In some cases leaves are arranged in a *spiral* up the stem or twig. This would seem to be a good pattern since one leaf does not shade the one below it. The leaves of the pussy willow are thus arranged. The leaves of many plants and trees are placed directly opposite each other, examples being honeysuckle, maple and ash. The fourth type of leaf arrangement is the *whorl*. In this case several leaves arise

Leaves are generally arranged on twigs and stems so that they shade each other as little as possible. Here are shown the three most common types of leaf arrangements. At the left is a silver maple twig having alternate *leaves. In the center is a pussy willow with leaves that* spiral *up the twig. At the right is a honeysuckle bush with* opposite *leaves.*

at one point, often at the tips of twigs. An example is the catalpa tree. The various kinds of leaf arrangements are of importance because they not only help botanists to classify plants but often help us to understand the biology of plant growth.

The spiral type of leaf arrangement offers many variations. Botanists have made careful studies of plants exhibiting this and have found out some very interesting things. If you will look closely at several kinds of tall plants, such as asters, garden weeds or trees, you will find that the leaf spirals of each one have certain special characteristics. The study of the way in which leaves are placed spirally around a stem is called *phyllotaxy* (pronounced file-o-taxy), a word that means literally "leaf arrangement." Each characteristic type of spiral leaf arrangement is called a *phyllotaxi,* but, for simplicity, we will call them "spirals." In order to understand how botanists classify the various kinds of spirals, let us assume that an ant begins crawling up an alder twig. It wishes to visit each leaf so it crawls upward in a spiral (which will be its shortest path) going from one leaf base to another. If we watch the ant we find that when it has reached the leaf directly above the one where it started it has already visited *three* leaves and circled the twig *once*. For this reason botanists call this leaf arrangement a *one-third spiral*. (If we wish to be very scientific, we can call it a *one-third phyllotaxi*.) In this type of spiral each leaf is placed one-third of the way around the stem or twig. Each one of these complete spirals, by the way, is called a *story*, and these arise one above the other like the stories in a building. Of course, they occur continously up the stem without a break, and each story ends with the leaf directly above the leaf where the count began, even though several spirals about the stem have been traced from leaf to leaf.

Let us next take an oak or willow twig and examine its leaf arrangement. In this case *two* spirals must be traced around the twig at the bases of *five* leaves before a leaf is reached that is located directly above the one where the count began. This is called a *two-fifths spiral* since the complete spiral passed *twice* around the twig and through the bases of *five* leaves, each of which is placed two-fifths of the way around the stem.

The above examples are quite easily understood, but there are other plants and trees in which the leaf spirals are much more complex. The leaf spiral of each kind of plant is usually the same and results from the manner in which the leaf buds develop at the growing tip of the shoot or twig. If you will study the picture of the models it will help you to understand this unusual feature of leaves.

This spiraling of leaves is of very practical importance to the plant since it assures each leaf of receiving its share of sunshine. It is interesting to note that different kinds of willows have their

Shown here are models of three simple kinds of leaf spiral arrangements, side view below and top view above. At the left is a one-half spiral, so called because each leaf is placed halfway around the stem. This is also called an alternate leaf arrangement, and is often found on horizontal twigs. At the center is a one-third spiral in which each leaf is placed one-third of the way around the stem, and their bases make one complete turn. In this case, one spiral of three leaves constitutes a story. At the right is a model of a two-fifths spiral. This is slightly more complicated in that each story consists of five leaves placed in two spirals around the stem. The top views show that in the one-half spiral the leaves are in two rows down the stem, the one-third spiral in three rows, and the two-fifths spiral in five rows.

leaves arranged in spirals of different types depending upon the size of the leaves. Those willows with broad leaves have their leaves arranged in fewer rows than the narrow-leaf kinds. This, of course, is directly related to the amount of shade cast by the leaves. Actually, there are some general conclusions that can be made as a result of these leaf studies. For instance, if leaves are broad and oval, as in the case of elm and redbud, they are usually arranged down the twigs in two rows, but if they are narrower and have short petioles or stems, as in the case of alder and beech, they are then arranged in five rows. It is all a matter of efficiency of shape and arrangement to allow sufficient light to reach each leaf.

Now you may wonder why we have gone into such detail in this discussion of leaf types—how they are arranged on the stem and how they serve the plant—but these are the characteristics that botanists look for when studying plants. In your excursions afield you should look for these features. The cultivation of such habits of observation will be very helpful to you, not only in the study of natural history but in other details of everyday life.

The leaves of many plants are cut by deep notches or even holes, which allow light to penetrate through to the lower leaves. In the case of the Japanese paper mulberry, only the upper leaves are deeply notched. This allows the sun to reach the leaves located at lower levels. These lower leaves are not notched. Certainly this is a very practical arrangement. The leaves of most trees are so arranged that the leaves in the interior of the trees receive their needed amount of sunlight sometime during the day, either morning or afternoon.

A number of plants solve the sunshine problem by having the stalks of the lower leaves much longer than those above. In this way they are thrust out where they can reach the light. Thus, many common plants are more or less cone-shaped, a form ideally suited to taking advantage of the sunlight that comes from above.

Plants and their leaves are, of course, continually under the influence of the sun because that is where they receive their energy to live and grow. The sun affects plants in many ways. Plants that live in the Tropics receive about twelve hours of sunlight a day while those living in Arctic regions are bathed in sunlight twenty-four hours a day during the short summer. This causes the latter to grow very rapidly, especially those plants that are native to Arctic regions. But there are other plants that are actually harmed by continuous light. Many plants, too, are influenced in their time of blooming by the length of the days. Violets, for example, normally bloom in the spring when the days are short. If they are covered during part of each day during summer, they will continue to bloom. Many plants in our climate fall into two classes. First, there are the long-day plants that bloom only during the long days of summer. The radish, iris, red clover, and evening primrose are in this category. The second type are the short-day plants whose blooms appear during the short days of spring and autumn. Examples are beggarticks, dahlia, ragweed and cosmos. The daisies and goldenrods of autumn also belong to this short-day class of plants. If autumn-blooming plants are covered during part of each day during summer, they can be made to bloom much earlier. It has been found that the temperature has little to do with the time of blooming so long as it is favorable to the plants' growth. The duration of exposure to sunlight is what makes the difference.

So far we have said nothing about *leaf-mosaics*. The next time you see an ivy covered wall, examine the leaves closely. If you do, you will notice that hardly a leaf completely shades the one next to it. This is because the leaves arrange themselves so as to take advantage of all the sunlight possible. The leaves thus form a mosaic that almost completely covers the wall. This fitting together of leaves is also found in many trees, especially in the outer branches where there are no leaves below to become shaded.

44

On the surface there seems to be no real logic in the size of most leaves. Most plants and trees bear small leaves, but a number of others "put all their eggs in one basket" and settle for a fewer number of large leaves. An example of this is the large-leaved magnolia or cucumber tree, whose leaves are often three feet or more in length and a foot wide. It would seem best from the plant's standpoint to have many smaller leaves, since the destruction of leaves through wind and insect damage would probably be less. On the other hand, anyone who has traveled in the Tropics knows that the huge leaves of the banana plant are almost always shredded by the wind yet seem perfectly healthy.

There are other characteristics of leaves that you will note if a number of different kinds are examined. The margins of some are smooth while others may be toothed or lobed. Tropical leaves usually have smooth or rounded edges while those of northern zones tend to have notched edges. The surfaces of some leaves are very hairy, as in the case of mullein, while in others the leaf surfaces are bare. Another important characteristic is in the arrangement of the veins. Leaves may be either *parallel-veined* or *net-veined*. As a matter of fact, the entire flowering plant kingdom is divided by botanists into the parallel-veined plants—such as grasses, bamboo, corn, lilies, and orchids —and the net-veined plants which includes most other kinds such as oaks, roses, and sunflowers.

Some leaf shapes we can explain, but it is pretty hopeless to attempt to explain all the varied shapes of leaves. They are the result of the genetic make-up of the plant, just as are the facial characteristics of human races. Still, as we have seen above, some leaves seem to be especially adapted to life under certain conditions. You will notice that many leaves end in points which hang downward. These points are called "drip tips," and they enable rain water to drain quickly off the leaves and not remain standing along the edges where disease-causing fungi and bac-

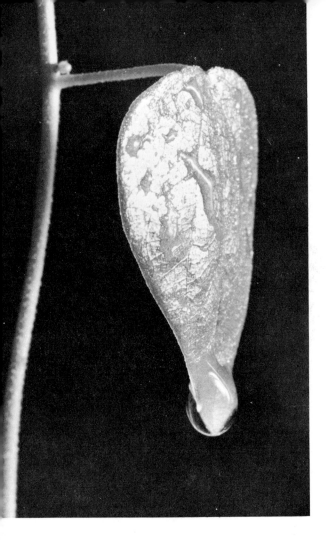

Many leaves have "drip tips" or pointed lower edges. This shape allows rain water to drip off quickly and not remain adhering to the leaf.

teria could enter and injure the leaf tissues. There are many other adaptations to life in special habitats. The petioles of the water hyacinth are swollen and filled with air to support the floating plant in water.

So far we have said nothing about the age of leaves. Plants, unlike animals, continue to grow throughout their lives. Some of the giant redwood trees of California are estimated to be 3,000 years old, yet they are still growing. These trees were saplings when the ancient Pharaohs ruled the Nile, but each year they still continue to grow and will no doubt continue to do so until some mishap such as a windstorm occurs to destroy them. By contrast, an animal grows to maturity and then continues to

46

live even though growth has stopped. As long as it lives, a plant continues to grow at its tip; thus the terminal leaves are always younger than the lower leaves. In other words, a plant is not the same age all over. It is interesting, too, that these young leaves are often shaped differently from those that grew earlier in the season. If you will examine the leaves of a larkspur plant you will find that those at the bottom are divided into fewer segments or parts than those at the top. If you pluck off successive leaves up the stem and lay them out on a table in proper order, you will discover an interesting thing. Each leaf is divided into a number of rays or segments, but each succeeding leaf up the stem has an increasing number of rays. You will find this same thing true of many other common plants, such as Ambrosia. Certain plants exhibit other differences between their young and old leaves. The older leaves at the base of a honeysuckle vine are divided by lobes, whereas all the leaves produced later are oval in shape. The cotton plant also shows a variation in leaf form as related to age. The older leaves at the bottom tend to be round while those higher and younger become increasingly lobed. It is interesting, too, that in some plants that produce side branches the sequence of leaf shapes from young to old starts over again with each side branch up the stem. This is true of the cotton plant.

Under the microscope there are other differences that can be detected between leaves of different ages. In the case of the tobacco plant, the lower leaves are the largest, and under the microscope it will be found that the cells in these leaves are larger than those in the leaves above. As one examines each successive leaf up the stalk, it will be found that there are fewer and smaller cells in each one. This adds up to the fact, of course, that the leaves themselves become smaller and smaller. This is in line with the previous statement that plants of this type tend to be cone-shaped so that each leaf receives its share of life-giving sunshine. To a plant, sunshine *is* life.

The age of leaves often determines their shapes. The honeysuckle vine shown here has several lobed leaves at the basal portion of its stems while the rest of the leaves are oval.

The leaves on an annual plant are not all the same age. In many cases the younger leaves at the top have more divisions than the older ones. Shown here are leaves from Ambrosia. Note that each succeeding leaf up the stem has more divisions.

CHAPTER 5

Leaf Defenses

*P*lants and animals are always in competition with each other. Plants furnish the food for the animal kingdom, yet they must defend themselves in order to survive. There are numerous ways in which plants and their leaves are protected. Some plants produce seeds in such enormous quantities that they apparently survive by sheer weight of numbers. In many other cases, however, plants and leaves have perfected clever ways of defending themselves from leaf-eating animals.

One of the most remarkable of all leaf defense mechanisms is found in the *taro* plant. I once spent some months in a laboratory in the Tropics where I had an opportunity to study the taro and observe its curious means of protecting itself. The taro is widely cultivated by natives in many tropical areas for its starchy roots. These tuberous roots must be cooked before being eaten, since both roots and leaves contain a most irritating substance that almost literally sets an animal's mouth on fire. (This same substance is also present in the large elephant-ear leaves—leaves that are never fed upon by deer or other browsing creatures.) One afternoon I examined a crushed portion of one of these taro leaves under a microscope and was amazed to find that the leaf tissues contained many tiny capsules, elongate in shape and filled with needle-like crystals. As I watched the crushed leaf under the microscope, these crystals could be seen to shoot, one

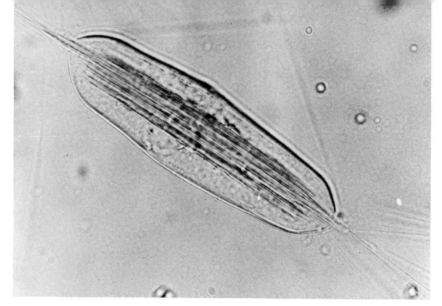

The leaves of the elephant-ear or taro plant contain microscopic capsules like this one which was photographed through a microscope. Needle-like crystals are "fired" into the mouth tissues of any animal attempting to eat the leaves. The capsule or "needle gun" shown here is in the process of discharging its stinging needles from both ends.

by one, out of their containing capsules like tiny arrows. As each needle-like crystal was "fired" the capsule recoiled like a dis-charged rifle. This, then, was the secret of the plant's defense. If one of these leaves is eaten and chewed up, the irritating crystals are "fired" into the sensitive tissues of the mouth caus-ing a burning sensation. Obviously, an animal would try eating a taro leaf but once! A deer, for example, would quickly learn to pass up taro leaves for more palatable forage.

This is just one example of the way in which a leaf renders itself unfit for food and thus protects itself from being devoured. There are thousands of other cases that could be mentioned. A good many leaves defend themselves by filling their tissues with poisonous substances quite capable of killing any creature that feeds upon them. Most poisonous plants belong to but a few plant families: lily family, pea family, buttercup family, spurge family, carrot family, nightshade family, heath family and daisy family. Of course, one should remember that most of the mem-bers of these families are non-poisonous and many of them are also important food plants—the onion belongs to the lily family, the common carrot to the carrot family, and potatoes, peppers and tomatoes to the nightshade family. While it is true, of course, that the leaves of most plants are harmless, it is never wise to chew or eat the leaf of any unknown plant.

There are many common examples of poisonous plants, some of them being found in almost every locality. It has been known for centuries, for instance, that the leaves of oleander are very toxic; chickens, sheep, cattle and horses have been poisoned by eating them. Human fatalities have also been reported. Other examples of poisonous ornamental plants are lily-of-the-valley, larkspur, foxglove, English ivy, narcissus, and castor-bean. Castor-beans are often chewed by children, causing severe illness or even death. The attractive beans are the chief offenders, but the leaves are also poisonous. This plant belongs to the spurge family. In the western United States range cattle are often poisoned by eating death camas, a member of the lily family that grows commonly on the ranges. Humans also have been fatally poisoned from eating the underground bulbs of this plant.

The nightshade or potato family contains a number of plants whose leaves are poisonous if eaten. Common jimson-weed, which was described earlier, contains a very toxic substance, and domestic animals and humans have often been poisoned. Other poisonous nightshades are henbane, belladonna and ground-cherry. Several members of the heath family, too, are poisonous, and domestic animals are sometimes killed by eating them. The heath family includes sheep-laurel or lambkill, mountain-laurel, and also rhododendron. Domestic animals soon learn to leave these dangerous plants alone, however, which proves that this method of leaf protection actually works.

Certainly, a discussion of poisonous plants should include mention of poison-hemlock, a plant made famous in history because it was probably the plant used to poison Socrates, the philosopher of ancient Greece. Unfortunately, this poisonous member of the parsley family has been introduced into the United States where it is quite common in many places. Human cases of poisoning often arise from eating the plant and from blowing whistles made from the hollow stems.

Other plants protect themselves by irritating substances that cause stinging sensations when they come in contact with the bare skin or cause blisters to appear later. Almost everyone is familiar with poison ivy, poison oak and poison sumac, but, fortunately, not everyone is sensitive to these evil plants. Even though you are apparently not sensitive to them, you should try to avoid direct contact. Once a rash develops from contact with the leaves of these pestiferous plants, sensitivity apparently increases. Unfortunately, a person sensitive to poison ivy does not become immune except through medical treatment, and authorities say that no one is completely immune. The leaves of these plants contain an oily substance which causes the inflammation and blistering which always is accompanied by intense itching.

There are many other plants that cause skin irritation when their leaves are handled. For example, nettles grow in many

The common nightshade plant protects itself in two ways. Its leaves are poisonous if eaten and they are also equipped with spines.

localities and one soon learns to leave them strictly alone since their leaves are armed with hairs or sharp spines that pierce the skin and cause intense itching. Certainly these plants have developed an effective means of defending their leaves against intruders, and no one who has ever handled a nettle can deny that plants sometimes do "bite back!"

The placing of poisons in leaves or arming them with nettle hairs or stinging spines may seem like a "sneaky" kind of protection. Other plants use more direct methods of defense. While working in tropical jungles, I once noticed heaps of black spiny brambles near the base of certain trees. They seemed to be dead, but examination showed that they were alive and connected with a slender vine that twined itself up the tree to the sunlight far above. More investigation showed that in the earth beneath the impenetrable mass of spiny vines were several potato-like tubers. This, obviously, was a clever method the plant had developed to protect its precious store of hidden food. I later learned that this plant is very aptly called the "spiny yam," not because the yams are spiny but because it uses spines to protect them.

The leaves and stem of the spurge nettle are covered with stinging spines that cause intense irritation if touched.

Cactus plants have their leaves changed into spines for protection. The work of the leaves is carried on by the fleshy stem.

Plants usually do not "invent" new structures or parts. They simply change some existing part to fulfill a new need. The thorns and spines of plants are actually stems, leaves or stipules that Nature has changed into protective devices. The spines of the black locust, for instance, are actually stipules (the leaf-like structures at the bases of leaves). You are, of course, familiar with the cactus spines, and these sharp daggers that so effectively protect the plant are, in truth, leaves. Long ages ago when Nature developed the cacti, the leaves lost their food-making functions and turned into spines. The work of food-making was assigned to the fleshy green stems, and that is the way the cactus tribe has lived ever since.

Sometimes leaves are merely equipped with spines along their veins and margins as in the case of the thistle. The holly tree has armed each of its leaves with spines which render them unfit for food. Some trees go a step farther and arm their trunks also with vicious daggers that no climbing creature could get past. The tree trunk and branches of the honey locust and the spiny palm are thus protected; these thorns are not only long and needle-sharp but often branched as well.

The honey locust tree has its trunk armed with vicious branched spines that few leaf-eating animals care to encounter.

The prickly leaves of the thistle are eaten by few creatures.

The spiny palm protects its leaves from climbing animals by a pincushion-like stem.

Century plants and yuccas are both members of the lily family, and as such, have long narrow leaves. But these plants defend themselves by having the tips of each of these sword-like leaves armed with sharp spines. In fact, the yuccas are often called Spanish daggers for this reason.

There are many other kinds of "porcupine plants" which secure protection from their enemies by spiny armaments, but there are still other tricks used by plants to protect themselves from enemies. Some of these are very clever, indeed. There are, in many parts of the world, plants that encourage the presence of stinging and biting ants, since the ants tend to prevent attacks by leaf-eating animals. Plants that enlist the aid of ants in this way are quite common in this country, and if you will examine elder, partridge pea, castor-bean, or the trumpet vine you will find usually, at the bases of the leaves, one or more small glandular structures. If you look at these glands carefully—especially with a hand lens—you will find that they are exuding a clear substance. Biologists call these glands *nectaries,* and the material they secrete *honeydew.* If you are lucky you will see a number of ants busily lapping up the sweet honeydew that the plant has

Many plants, such as this elderberry, have nectaries which secrete a sweet substance loved by ants. The presence of the ants discourages attacks by leaf-eating creatures.

made available to them. The ants, of course, do not know why the tempting nectar is being offered them, and they do not care. They are only interested in the fact that it is available. Most ants, of course, do not feed directly upon plants so the plants are not harmed, but ants are enemies of caterpillars and beetles, and these insects do destroy leaves. So, by attracting a volunteer army of ants, the plants are more or less protected. Certainly this is a most interesting relationship that has developed between ants and some common plants.

Now listen to the story of the bull-horn acacia tree that grows in Mexico and Central America. This amazing tree maintains a standing ant army that defends it against all comers including man.

In the tropical regions, where the bull-horn acacias grow, the chief enemy of leaves are the leaf-cutting or *Atta* ants that dwell in large underground cavities. These leaf-cutters make foraging expeditions above ground for the purpose of gathering leaves which they cut up and carry back to their nests. Here, in the damp underground tunnels, the leaves are used as a compost upon which is grown a type of fungus that is the food of the

The Mexican acacia tree grows hollow, twin thorns in which vicious stinging ants live. These ants drive away leaf-eating animals. Note entrance hole made by ants in the thorn at the right.

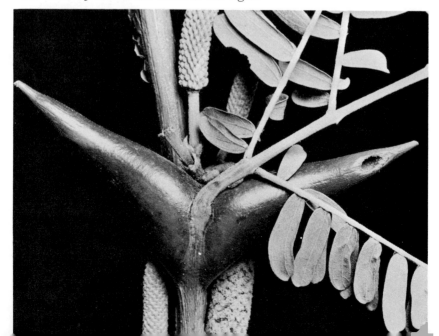

This is a close-up of the Mexican or bull-horn acacia thorn and one of its protective ants at the entrance into the hollow thorn.

ants. The colonies of leaf-cutting ants are very large, and great quantities of fresh leaves are constantly needed to keep the underground mushroom gardens growing. As a result, the leaf-cutters have been known to strip a tree of its leaves completely in a single night. The leaf-cutting *Atta* ants are not particular about what leaves they gather. Almost any kind will do, including those of the bull-horn acacia. But the bull-horn acacia has enlisted the aid of another kind of ant to protect its precious foliage.

The stipules at the base of each acacia leaf have been changed by Nature into large hollow thorns that resemble bull horns. These thorns make perfect homes—perhaps we should say barracks—for *Pseudomyrma* (pronounced sood-o-mer-ma) ants. These ants are relatively small and slender, but they have vicious stings. Into one tip of each pair of thorns the *Pseudomyrmas* cut a round entrance and establish headquarters. The walls of the thorn are hard, and the ants are well protected from the weather. So much for living quarters, but the acacia tree also provides its ant army with food. Near the base of each leaf there is located a row of crater-like nectaries where the ants can obtain nourishment. The ants thus have a place to live and a nearby source of food, but under such conditions they would probably become lazy and not patrol the leaves on the lookout for leaf-cutting enemies, especially their cousins, the *Atta* ants. Fortunately, the acacia tree has found a way to entice its army of *Pseudomyrmas* out to each leaflet. At the tip of each small leaflet there is produced a tiny fruit-like body that ants find most palatable. As a result, they patrol the leaves constantly, seeking this fruit. Sometimes they find a ripe one, and sometimes they do not, but each leaf of the acacia is always guarded by a number of *Pseudomyrma* ants, each armed with a vicious sting. Certainly it would be difficult for a tree to find more effective means of protecting its foliage.

One of the most unusual "twists" in botany is the case of the pitcher plant that has insect-catching leaves which literally trap unsuspecting insects inside them. Near the leaves are hollow tendrils within which lives a certain kind of ant, unmolested by the plant. These ants protect the plant by driving off leaf-eating animals just as the *Pseudomyrma* ants do in the case of the bull-horn acacia. But, on the other hand, the cannibal-like pitcher plant captures and digests *other* insects in its hollow leaves.

A close-up of the hairs on the lower surface of a leaf. Some leaves are covered with such dense growths of hair that leaf-eating insects leave them alone.

CHAPTER 6

Leaves Alive

*M*ost of us think of plants and their leaves as being stationary objects, without power of movement. Thus, it may come as a surprise to you to learn that, in addition to normal growth, most plants and leaves are almost continually moving in slow motion even when there is no breeze blowing. The movements of animals, of course, are more obvious because they are much more rapid.

There are a number of ways in which plant and leaf movements may be seen. Perhaps the most spectacular of these is by means of time-lapse photography. In this process a movie camera is focused upon a plant and timed in such a way that one picture is taken every hour or every three hours, or any other set interval. When the film is developed and then projected upon a movie screen at the usual rate of about sixteen pictures per second, any movement of the plant is thus speeded up tremendously, and we see that the plant is almost never still. Suppose the camera is focused upon a rose bush and set to take pictures every few hours while a rose bud slowly opens into a full-blown flower and then withers petal by petal. When we view the finished film the flower seems to open miraculously, nod in the air and then wither and droop all in the space of a few minutes. A time-lapse camera can also be focused upon a leaf and its movements observed. The leaf will be seen to open

61

The leaves of many plants exhibit "sleep movements"; that is, the leaves fold up during the night or in darkness. The leaflets of this cassia plant show the folded position of the leaflets in "sleep."

Oxalis or wood sorrel leaves fold up at night and spread out in the sun during the day. The leaf at the left is "asleep" while the one at the right is "awake."

and close as night and day succeed each other, and to change its angle as it follows the sun across the sky.

Most of us cannot afford expensive time-lapse cameras, but we can nevertheless make observations of plant movements. Some afternoon look at a sunflower. Its "face" is turned toward the west as it follows the setting sun. If you look at this same flower the next morning, you will find that the flower then faces east toward the rising sun. Oxalis is a common plant of the flower garden. If you observe it during the daylight hours, you will find that each of its three-parted leaves is spread flat to catch the rays of the sun, but if you observe the leaves at night with a flashlight, you will find that the leaflets are folded in "sleep." If you plant an oxalis plant in a pot you can make interesting observations of its *sleep movements.* Place such a potted plant in a darkened room and then observe it after an hour. You will find that the leaves have "gone to sleep" even in the middle of the day. The leaves of some acacia plants are also very sensitive to light. Some kinds of these plants have leaves which begin to close even when a dark cloud comes across the face of the sun. I was once camped in a tropical jungle and at night when I walked down a path with a flashlight I noticed some strange-looking plants. When I looked for these plants again the next day they were apparently gone. The next night they were back again! Upon further investigation it was found that these mysterious plants were a type of acacia whose leaves fold up at dusk in such a way as to change the looks of the plants entirely.

There are many common plants that exhibit these "sleep movements." The leaves of the jewelweed droop at night and are elevated during the day. Pigweed leaves face the sun during the day and turn on their edges at night. The circular leaves of the common nasturtium also tip up on their edges at night.

Perhaps the most remarkable of these plant movements are those exhibited by the "telegraph plant" of Bengal. The leaflets of this plant are constantly in motion all day for no apparent reason. The leaves move up and down and also in circles, and while the leaflets on one side of the stem are rising, those on the opposite side are lowering. These leaf movements are most noticeable when the sun is shining.

Biologists have found that these leaf movements are caused in several different ways. Within growing plants, and especially at their tips, there are produced certain growth-regulating substances called *auxins*. These are something like the chemical regulators or *hormones* found in animals. Auxins tend to stimulate plant growth. Now when sunlight falls upon a leaf the light reduces the amount of auxin on the upper surface or makes the tissues less sensitive to it and the growth of the upper surface of the leaf and its stem or petiole is slowed down. The result is that the leaf bends upward. This is the way botanists explain the up-and-down sleep movements of many leaves. They have also found that when bean seedlings are grown in continuous

64

darkness their leaves do not show these sleep movements. This was to be expected since the up-and-down movements of the leaves apparently result from alternating day and night. Then, amazingly, it was discovered that if these same bean plants were given only a short period of bright light their leaves began exhibiting a regular 24-hour sleep-movement rhythm! In other words, their leaves followed a schedule of day and night rising and lowering, even though they were kept in complete darkness again after the brief exposure to light. This rhythm continued for several days. Why? The truth is that scientists do not really know. For millions of years plants and animals have been adjusted to a daily rhythm governed by the rotation of the earth. Within many plants and animals there appear to be built-in clocks that govern their daily activities just as watches govern our own lives. How these clocks work is one of the unsolved riddles of biology.

Everyone is familiar with the fact that a plant bends or grows toward a source of light such as that from a window. Usually we assume that the plant seeks the light because it needs the sunshine to help it grow. This sounds reasonable, but, unfortunately, it is not so. As we saw above, sunlight slows down the flow of growth-stimulating auxins; thus the side of the plant stem toward the light tends to grow more slowly than the dark side. This unequal growth rate of the two sides of the stem causes the plant to bend toward the light. Of course, the end result is that the plant eventually does reach the light, but the plant does not grow toward the light because it "wants" to do so.

These strange chemical growth-regulating auxins are mostly produced at the growing tip of the plant. They are, of course, liquid and flow downward through the stem causing the plant to do a number of things. For instance, if you tip a potted plant on its side even in complete darkness the stem will slowly bend upward so that it eventually becomes vertical again. This is the normal position of the plant, but how did the plant "know"

Most leaves are "attracted" to light and are thus said to be positively photo-tropic. These bean seedlings were grown near a light bulb and, as can be seen, they grew toward the source of light.

which way was up in the darkness? In the darkness there was no sunlight to influence the flow of auxin so this substance flowed down the stem from the growing tip. But it tended to flow down the lower side in larger amounts, with the result that the cells on the lower side of the stem were stimulated and grew faster. This caused the stem to bend upward. As soon as the stem reached a vertical position the auxin began flowing down all sides in equal amounts and the stem continued to grow straight up. It grew straight because its growing cells were stimulated equally on all sides.

Auxins also affect the manner in which certain climbing vines grow. You may have noticed how evenly the leaves of ivy are spread out against a wall, forming a leaf-mosaic. There seems to be very little overlapping. This spacing of the leaves results from the same mechanism by which stems bend toward the light. When an ivy leaf is shaded by another leaf, it bends toward the light and the wall becomes covered by a mosaic of evenly spaced leaves.

66

We have seen how plants and their leaves turn toward the sun and how some leaves exhibit "sleep movements" caused by growth-regulating auxins. Actually, two different kinds of sleep movements occur in leaves. We have already considered the type in which leaves merely move up and down in daylight and darkness. There is another type of "sleep movement" in which leaflets fold tightly together for the night. Mimosa, acacia, partridge pea and some other pea plants do this. If a partridge pea is examined during the daylight hours its leaflets are spread flat to capture the sun's rays. But after the sun has set, and it is growing dark, the tiny leaflets begin to fold up for the night and will remain pressed tightly together in "sleep." At sunrise they will slowly open again. Scientists have found that this remarkable leaflet closing is brought about in an interesting way.

At the base of each small leaflet there is a cushion-like swelling. During the daylight hours while the leaves are actively at work producing starch, these cushions are swollen with water and support the leaflets, but when darkness comes they lose their water and the leaflets close. Just how this benefits the plant botanists are not agreed. Perhaps the closing of the leaves helps the plant conserve moisture.

There are some plants whose leaflets fold up whenever they are disturbed, even in broad daylight. These are called "sensitive plants," and their leaflets close very rapidly at any sudden jar. The closing mechanism in these sensitive plants is very similar to that found in the partridge pea, but they move much faster. Although the leaflets of the sensitive plants close within a second or so, they usually require several minutes to open again.

It is always interesting to try to find the reason behind everything in nature. So we might ask, "Why do sensitive plants close their leaves when the plant is disturbed?" For protection, would be a sound answer. When the leaves are expanded the plant is very conspicuous and perhaps a grazing animal would consider

The leaflets of the sensitive brier are very sensitive to touch. If the vine or brier is touched or shaken, all the leaflets will suddenly fold up.

Here we see the same sensitive brier a few seconds after it was shaken. The leaflets have all folded up, causing the plant almost to disappear.

it good to eat. After the leaflets all close, however, little is seen except the bare stems. As a matter of fact, one kind, the sensitive brier, almost disappears when its leaflets suddenly fold up.

Probably the most fascinating of all leaf movements are found in the Venus flytrap, a marsh-loving plant found only in the Carolinas of the United States. In this plant the leaves are hinged along the mid-rib and when any insect crawls across it the leaf quickly folds together, imprisoning the unlucky insect. The insect is then digested and absorbed by the cannibal-like plant. These, and other insect-eating plants, are discussed in detail in another chapter.

Botanists often speak of the responses of plants and leaves to outside stimuli, such as light and gravity, as *tropisms*. Thus, they call the bending of a plant toward the light *photo-tropism,* and this may be either negative or positive depending on whether the plant bends toward the light or away from it. The roots of plants are negatively photo-tropic since they bend away from the light. Plant stems are spoken of as being negatively *geo-tropic* because they resist the pull of gravity. Roots are, of course, positively *geo-tropic*. If this were not so a farmer would have to plant each seed with its "root end" downward. Fortunately, the stem always grows up and the roots always grow down regardless of which way the seed is planted.

There are many types of tropisms. Most climbing vines and tendrils respond positively to touch. This is called *thigmo-tropism*. Whenever a vine or tendril touches any object it "tries" to twine around it. Tendrils are usually modified leaves or branches, and they serve to support the growing plant. This climbing habit is found in many plants including grapes, gourds and peas. The tendrils of some of these plants twine about a supporting object—a fence or trellis—very rapidly, a complete coil often requiring but a few minutes.

Probably the first person to make extensive studies of plant movements was Charles Darwin, the great naturalist. As a mat-

Plants respond to gravity or geo-tropism as well as to light. These sprouting grains of corn were placed in different positions, yet the young stems all grew upward and the roots all grew downward.

ter of fact, he reported the results of his studies in a book consisting of more than five hundred pages. You would find this old volume most interesting. It is entitled *Power of Movement in Plants* and can usually be found in most large libraries. Among the plant movements studied by Mr. Darwin were the growth movements of stems. He found that the stems of most growing plants sway about in circles as they grow. He called this *circumnutation* and it is a phenomenon that you can easily observe for yourself. Obtain some vigorously growing potted plant—a bean seedling will do—and place a piece of window

70

glass several inches above it so that the glass is supported in a horizontal position on four stakes. Now, with a wax pencil, make a mark on the glass directly above the growing tip of the plant. Record the time, and make additional marks every few hours. In this way you can trace the movements of the plant, and you will be surprised how much it moves about within the space of a few days. You will also find that the tip of the plant tends to move in circles. Just why a plant does this is not fully understood. Anyway, we have a name for it, thanks to Charles Darwin.

There is an old belief that vines in the Northern Hemisphere twine in one direction and those in the Southern Hemisphere in the other direction. This is not true, and you can easily prove the fallacy of this by making a few first-hand observations. Some vines

Leaves must have sunlight in order to manufacture food. Plants growing in dark tropical jungles push upward to the sunshine.

Some vines twine to the left and others to the right. This smilax vine is an example of one that twines to the right.

twine one way and some the other, and a few vines twine *both* ways. Most bean, pea and smilax plants twine to the right, but supple-jack and hop vines twine toward the left. The common bitter-sweet turns in both directions. It is interesting also that these vines revolve about a supporting twig or vine at different rates. For instance, a hop vine requires about two hours for one revolution; the trumpet vine about six and a half hours; and honeysuckle eight hours. In some plants, such as the passion-flower, the tendrils bend very rapidly. If a tendril of one of these plants is touched, it will begin to curl within a minute but will straighten out again if the object touching it is removed.

Perhaps the most remarkable of all leaf movements are those exhibited by the compass plant of our western prairies. This is a member of the daisy family having its leaves growing upon an erect stalk. These leaves, however, are not spread with their surfaces level with the ground but stand on edge and point north and south so that the plant appears to be flat. By having their leaves arranged in this fashion, they always face the morning and afternoon sun. This vertical position also helps to protect the leaves from the hot drying rays of the prairie sun at mid-day since it strikes only their edges at that time. Strangely, this plant, when growing in shady meadows, turns its leaves to a level position like any other plant. It is said that early travelers on the prairies often used these unusual plants to tell direction in place of a magnetic compass.

The honeysuckle vine is an example of a "left-handed" vine. It twines to the left.

When an insect crawls—or is placed—in the leaf-trap of the Venus flytrap, the leaf snaps shut and captures the insect. It is then digested.

CHAPTER 7

Cannibal Leaves

Plants put their leaves to almost every conceivable use, in addition to the usual one of food manufacture. Probably the strangest leaves of all, however, are those that are used as traps to capture insects. In the world there are about five hundred different kinds of these plants, most of which grow in marshy areas that are apparently deficient in nitrogen. Nitrogen is, as you may know, one of the most important elements for plant growth. The bodies of all animals contain a lot of nitrogen, and these cannibal plants have developed the unique habit of capturing and digesting small creatures to provide this important part of their diet. When a farmer plants his crops, he usually also fertilizes the soil to make the crop plants grow better. One of the important elements he adds to the soil is nitrogen in the form of nitrate. Thus, plants that grow where the soil does not contain enough nitrogen must get it somewhere else if they are to thrive. The cannibal plants obtain it from insects they capture and digest.

Perhaps the most spectacular of these insect-eating plants are the Venus flytraps, found growing only in bogs along the coastal areas of the Carolinas. Just why they do not grow anywhere else is something of a mystery. Evidently these unusual plants require very special conditions for growth that are found only in that area. They can be grown for a short while in a glass box or aquarium, but in time they always wither away and die when removed from their native bogs.

The Venus flytrap is a small plant, hardly over six inches in diameter with a rosette of leaves arising around a central root. The flower is white or yellowish and is borne on a stalk that grows up from the center of the plant. It is the leaves, of course, that are of interest to us here. Each one is more or less tongue-shaped with its end portion oval and hinged down the center. The inner surfaces of the mature leaves are orange-red, but the most conspicuous thing about them are the long sharp teeth extending out from the margins. If you have an opportunity to examine one of these trap-leaves closely you will find that there are four small bristles located in the red central portion of the leaf. These are the "trigger hairs," but if you touch just one of these nothing happens. You must touch at least two of them, one after another, before the leaf snaps shut. Nature has designed the leaf-trap in this way so that a blade of grass, for instance, brushing against the leaf will usually not trip it. On the other hand, when an ant or other small insect crawls across the leaf it touches one and then another of the trigger hairs and the leaf snaps shut trapping the insect. Actually, the Venus flytrap does not depend on chance in its insect trapping. The leaf evidently secretes an attractive substance that lures the insects to their dooms between the jaws of the leaf-traps. Once an insect is captured the leaf-trap holds it tightly for a week or two until the softer parts of its body are all digested and absorbed by the plant. At the end of this time the leaf slowly opens, and the remaining dried portion of the insect blows away. The plant is now ready to trap more game.

You can easily fool the Venus flytrap by brushing the trigger hairs with a straw. The leaf-trap will snap shut, but, since nothing is captured, it will open again in about fifteen minutes. Now you might like to know what makes the leaf-traps of the Venus flytrap close when the trigger hairs are touched. As a matter of fact, so would a lot of scientists who have studied them. They have found out many interesting things about the leaf-traps, but they still do not agree as to just what makes them close. Plants, of course, do not have muscles or nerves like animals, so there must be some other explanation. Some scientists believe that the power for snapping the leaf shut comes from released water pressure in the cells along the center, but others believe that the leaf grows unequally and that a tension or strain is created causing the trap to shut when it is stimulated by any small creature crawling across it. You may also be interested in knowing that scientists have connected these leaves to very sensitive electrical instruments and found that when a leaf-trap snaps shut a small electric current is created. Perhaps, after all, the leaf does have something similar to an animal's nerves, since the nervous impulses of animals are really electrical in nature.

While the Venus flytrap grows only in the Carolina bogs of the United States, there is a plant in Europe with quite similar habits. Strangely, however, this European trap plant dwells *underwater!* It is found in quiet water just below the surface and is called *Aldrovanda* (pronounced all-dro-van-da). The leaf-traps of this plant more or less resemble those of the Venus flytrap but are much smaller. They also possess trigger hairs, and their food consists of small *aquatic* or water creatures.

Here in the United States is found a common water plant that also captures small aquatic creatures such as water-fleas or even mosquito wigglers. Its trapping method, however, is different from either the Venus flytrap or the European water plant. You may have seen these plants since they are actually quite common in ponds. Botanists call them *bladderworts*, a name meaning "bladder-plant." (The name *wort* is found in many plant names and is an old word for "plant.") The name in this case is very appropriate since these floating plants have many small bladder-like structures along the stems, each about an eighth of an inch long. If you examine one of these bladders under a

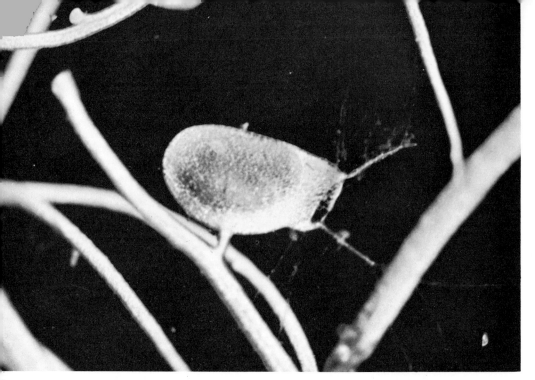

One of the most unusual of the cannibal plants is the bladderwort *which grows under water and catches and digests tiny aquatic creatures. When any small animal touches one of the trigger hairs it is sucked into the bulb-like trap and digested.*

lens, you will see that one end has a hinged lip or trap door. When this lid is in the closed position, it is watertight and the water pressure inside becomes less than that outside. Just outside the trap door there are sensitive trigger hairs, and when a tiny creature—even a microscopic *paramecium*—touches these the lip snaps open and water is sucked in, carrying the unfortunate animal with it. There can be no doubt that these tiny traps are efficient since almost every one examined contains some "game."

So far we have talked about the leaves that snap shut on their game, but there is another class of plants that do their "trapping" with glue in the same way that we catch flies with sticky flypaper. The most common of these "flypaper plants" are the sundews that grow in small rosettes somewhat like Venus flytraps. Their trapping method, however, is quite different. The entire plant is hardly over an inch in diameter and is reddish in color. Each small leaf is covered with numerous tentacles, each tipped with a shining globule of glue. Apparently, insects of small size, such as gnats, are attracted to these leaves and become helplessly ensnared in the glue. Within a few hours the leaf and the nearby tentacles bend over and pin the insect down and digest it. In my laboratory I have several of these interesting little plants. One day I placed a leafhopper on one of the leaves. The next morning when I examined the sundew plant and photographed it, the leaf had curled over and the glue-tipped tentacles had pinned the leafhopper down securely. Later the leaf of this tiny cannibal plant slowly digested the insect and absorbed its nourishment.

Probably the most widely distributed of these "flypaper plants" is *Pinguicula* (pronounced pen-guik-u-la) or butterwort. (Notice here again the use of *wort*.) The name actually means "butter plant," so called because its leaves have been

The butterwort plant captures insects on its adhesive leaves. When an insect becomes trapped on one of the sticky leaves, the edge of the leaf then curls over and digests the insect.

This leafhopper was "captured" by the adhesive ten-tacles on a sundew leaf. Each tentacle is tipped with a globule of glue.

A few hours later the sundew leaf had bent over and the leafhopper was firmly grasped, to be slowly di-gested by the cannibal leaf.

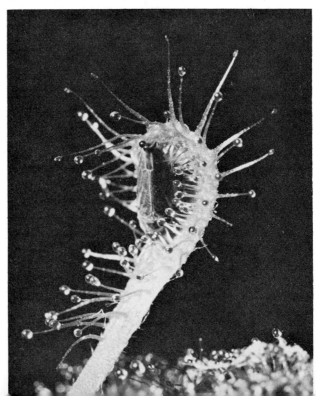

used for centuries in Scandinavian countries to treat milk for the production of a special dish. We know now that the leaves of butterwort contain a substance similar to rennet that coagulates fresh milk.

The leaves of the butterwort plant are pale green and covered with a sticky substance. Their outer edges curl inward. When insects alight upon the sticky leaves, they are trapped by the glue, and the edge of the leaf slowly curls over and pins the creature down. Protein-dissolving enzymes are then poured upon it, and digestion takes place, as in the case of the other cannibal leaves.

So far we have considered only those cannibal leaves that have moving parts by which insects are trapped. Let us next investigate other kinds of leaves that are successful in catching insect game but which have no moving parts at all. These are the pitcher plants, and they are even more widely distributed than the other kinds, being found in many parts of the world. In the United States they occur in the north-central portion of the country ranging all the way into Canada. Other kinds thrive in marshy coastal areas from New Jersey to Louisiana. In the West they are found in both California and Oregon. One American species (kind) has been successfully introduced into Switzerland.

The pitcher plants all have one feature in common. Their leaves, instead of being flat blades, are hollow and shaped like cornucopias. Some of these insect-catching leaves stand erect while others lie flat on the ground. Most of them have their tips formed into hoods that curve up or over the tops of the leaf cavity. In the case of the northern pitcher plant, the inner surface of this hood is set with numerous sharp spines and when an insect once begins crawling over it, the spines prevent it from escaping. The doomed creature has no choice but to continue crawling on into the narrowing leaf tube where more spines prevent escape. Eventually the insect can go no farther and is

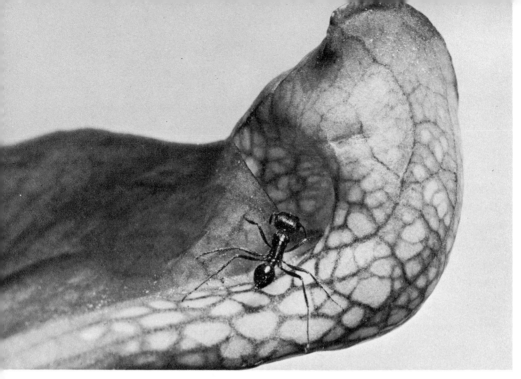

The leaves of this pitcher plant resemble a canoe. When an ant enters the opening under the "prow" at the right, it will find itself in a chamber with a passage leading back through the lower portion of the hollow leaf. (See next photograph.)

trapped. The digestive juices of the leaf then dissolve and absorb the nitrogenous materials out of the insect's body.

Many of the pitcher plants are very pretty, and their blooms are large and attractive, being either yellow or red. Some kinds of pitcher plants found in the eastern coastal area grow with their hollow leaves straight up, each with a hood or canopy that curves gracefully over the open top. These trumpet-like leaves vary in color from green to red, and they are often marked with spots. Some of these spots, especially those on the hood, are transparent, and when insects trapped inside the hollow leaf attempt to fly out they merely bang against the transparent "windows" and tumble back into the narrow throat of the cannibal leaf. Incidentally, the hoods or canopies of these leaves are threaded with red, branching veins that remind one even more of animals.

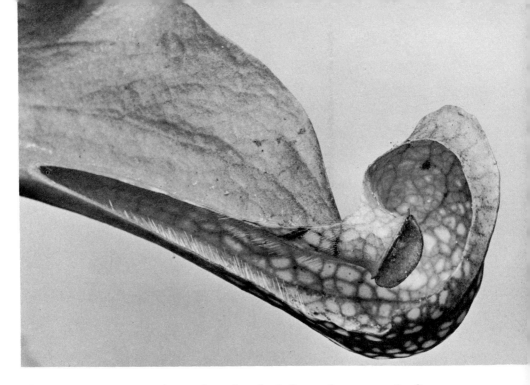

This cut-a-way view of the pitcher plant leaf shows the passage leading toward the left. Once an insect such as an ant begins crawling up this passage, the spines prevent it from escaping. The leaf then digests and absorbs the unfortunate insect.

The pitcher plants, like the Venus flytrap and sundew, apparently secrete a substance that it very attractive to flies, moths, beetles and ants, and some of these insects are almost always flying or crawling about the leaf-traps. Now and then one of the insects investigates too closely and tumbles in. Usually there is but little chance of escape since the lower portion of the hollow leaf is filled with water containing a narcotic material that paralyzes the insects once they have fallen in. The captured prey, of course, is digested and absorbed as in the case of the other cannibal plants.

If one takes the trouble to cut open a number of pitcher plant leaves it is soon realized just how efficient the leaf-traps really are. Almost every one will be found to contain a number of insects, and in some cases the leaves are completely filled with insect remains.

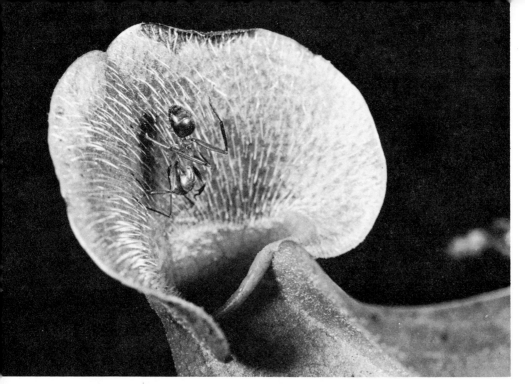

Here is another pitcher plant, the variety found in the north-central United States and Canada. The ant, crawling into the opening, is trapped by the spines and cannot escape.

We have now seen how these ingenious cannibal leaves capture and eat insects, so it may surprise you to learn that there are a few kinds of insects that actually make their homes safely within the lethal leaf-traps of the pitcher plants. There are small brownish moths that lay their eggs in the leaves of the pitcher plants. They will lay their eggs nowhere else. When these eggs hatch, the caterpillars feed upon the nutritious leaves, often completely destroying them. Then, when the caterpillar is about ready to spin its cocoon it cuts a narrow groove around the inside wall of the leaf-trap and spins a web of silk across the hollow. The groove causes the top portion of the leaf pitcher to collapse and the silken web seals the opening against any intruder. The caterpillar then spins its cocoon and transforms into the pupal or inactive stage. In time the adult moth emerges from the cocoon and flies away. If it is a female, she will mate and lay her eggs in other leaf pitchers.

84

The pitcher plant moths are not the only insects that have found safe havens in the deadly leaf traps, however. We have already noted that the leaf-traps of the pitcher plants are usually partly filled with water into which the unfortunate insect prey tumble. It is odd, therefore, to learn that there is also a mosquito that flies down into the dangerous leaf-trap and lays her eggs in the hidden pool of water. After laying her eggs she flies out safely and lays eggs in other pitcher plant leaf pools. The eggs, which she risked her life to lay, soon hatch into wigglers or *larvae* which grow to maturity inside the cannibal leaf where most other creatures are killed and eaten. How they can do this is one of the strange and unexplained riddles of biology.

This strange looking caterpillar lives safely inside the leaves of pitcher plants where other insects are killed and digested.

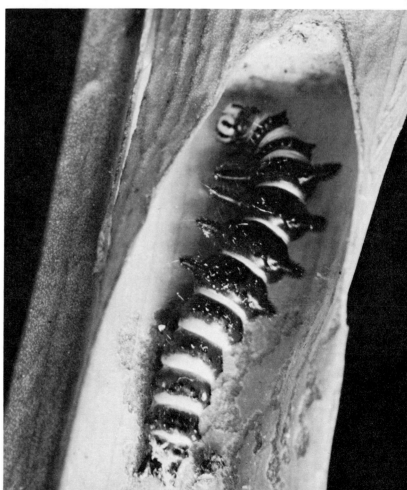

This picture looks like an aerial view of an African village, but it is actually a close-up of insect galls on a hickory leaf.

CHAPTER 8

Leaf Palaces

$\mathcal{I}$t has been said that leaves feed the world, and this, of course, is literally true. But it is also true that leaves, directly, or indirectly, *house* the world. The houses of many of the world's people are still built of woven and thatched palm fronds. Anyone who has resided or lived in tropical lands has seen the neat homes so cunningly built by natives out of local materials obtained directly from the surrounding jungles. These homes are practical and sanitary, and admirably adapted to hot climates. When one enters a native home covered with six inches of nipa (pronounced nee-pa) palm thatch, it is almost like entering an air-conditioned house. The thick over-lapping layers of palm fronds form an excellent insulation against the rays of the tropical sun, even at mid-day. The nipa palm, by the way, is an unusual palm that grows along the margins of streams. Its trunk, instead of growing straight up, creeps under the mud sending its huge, graceful fronds or leaves up into the air. They are ideal for use as thatching material.

The human race has been using plant materials for home construction since the days of the cave man. Early American settlers built log cabins, but, later, the logs were replaced by sawed lumber. In recent years the sawed lumber has been replaced to a certain extent by "lumber" consisting of wood pulp that has been chemically treated and pressed into hard sheets suitable for constructing walls and other parts of a house. But whether we use leaves or fronds directly or the compressed fiber of trees for home construction, we are still taking advantage of the toil of the busy leaves.

As one might expect, other creatures, too, use plant leaves to shield themselves from weather and enemies. In East Indian islands there are some unusual ants that "sew" plant leaves together to form a snug nest. What is most unusual about these ants, however, is the manner in which they "sew" these leaves together. Adult ants cannot secrete silk. Silk secretion is confined to the larvae, or young, that use it for spinning their cocoons. As a result, these remarkable ants use their silk-spinning larvae like bobbins which they hold in their jaws and pass back and forth from one leaf to another, gradually pulling them together until a tight leaf nest is formed.

One never thinks of the members of the grasshopper and cricket tribe as being adept at any sort of home or shelter construction. In fact, the old fable of the lazy grasshopper and the industrious ant shows our attitude regarding the grasshopper and cricket clan. Thus, it may surprise you to know that there is a cricket found in the eastern United States that has developed the silk-secreting habit and uses its silk to "sew" leaves into neat tubes within which it hides during the daylight hours when cricket-hunting birds are active. Strangely, this unusual cricket emerges at dusk to feed upon aphids or plant lice.

Caterpillars or young of many moths, of course, dwell within rolled-up leaves, emerging only to feed on nearby foliage. Such caterpillars are called "leaf-rollers" and many of them are of economic importance. A common example is the grape leaf-roller, a strikingly marked black and white moth whose larvae dwell within rolled-up grape leaves. Actually, some caterpillars merely fold the edges of leaves over and fasten them down with silk. These kinds are usually called "leaf-folders" as contrasted to the "leaf-rollers." Another insect, the pine tube

Here a leaf-rolling cricket "sews" a leaf together to form a leaf tent within which it will hide. This is a very unusual habit of the cricket tribe.

builder, lives within a neat tube which it constructs by cementing several pine needles together. You may have read how the larva of the large Promethea moth constructs its cocoon within a folded leaf which it first fastens securely to the twig to prevent its falling during the winter.

Some spiders, too, live in homes fabricated from leaves. One spider very cleverly folds a blade of grass over to form a box-like cell within which it hides.

Some insects live not only upon leaves but actually inside them. There are many insects that live and feed between the layers of thin leaves. Of course, all of these insects are very tiny since such living quarters are not roomy. They are called "leaf-miners" and spend all or a part of their lives between the upper and lower surfaces of various leaves. You have probably seen these "mines" made in leaves by insects as they tunneled through the tissues. Some of these tunnels form interesting patterns where the small larvae have circled about in the leaf,

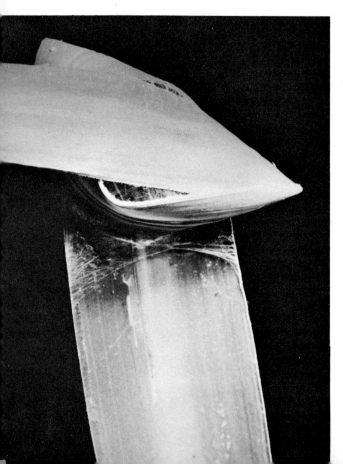

This clever cell was constructed by a spider by bending a blade of grass about in a certain way and fastening it together with silk.

Leaf-mining insects tunnel between the upper and lower surfaces of many leaves. This "x-ray" of a bean leaf shows such a tunnel or leaf mine. Note how each tunnel gradually widened as the insect grew.

feeding as they tunneled along. There is a leaf-miner in the Northwest that makes very pretty patterns in quaking aspen leaves. If you trace one of these leaf mines carefully, you will notice that the mine is very narrow at one end and wide at the other end. This is because the mine was naturally very narrow when the miner was small. As it tunneled along and increased in size, however, the mine gradually became wider. As a general rule, the mines made in leaves by insects are characteristic for each kind of insect. The leaf-mining insects thus leave their signatures or trademarks in the leaves where they have lived and fed.

Animals of all sorts feed directly or indirectly upon leaves. This ranges from cattle feeding on grass to our habit of eating

91

spinach and cabbage. A little more unusual is the use made of leaves by the strange leaf-cutting ants of the American Tropics. These are the *Atta* ants, which are the enemies of the bull-horn acacia and other plants, and they are also found in Texas and Louisiana. Everywhere they turn up they are considered to be serious pests because of their leaf-gathering habit.

When naturalists first visited the areas in the American Tropics where these ants abound, and saw the long ant columns carrying pieces of leaves, they thought the leaves were being used to thatch or line their nests. Eventually, however, it was discovered that the *Atta* ants actually carry the leaves far underground to large cavities where they are converted into compost upon which the ants grow fungi. It is upon this fungus that the ants feed. The ants are thus, in truth, mushroom growers!

There are many different relationships between leaves and animals, but perhaps the most remarkable of all is the story of the insects that cause leaves to grow special homes for them. There are many different kinds of these insects, some of which are tiny wasps, while others are plant lice or members of the fly family.

The structures these insects produce on leaves and other parts of plants are called *galls,* but just how the insects cause the plants to form them is unknown as yet. Let us take, as an example, the oak leaf gall. In early summer or spring while the leaves are still growing the tiny gall wasp lays her egg in an oak leaf. In time this egg hatches into a minute grub or larva. Now as a result of some chemical substance which the larva secretes as it grows, or perhaps because of mechanical irritation, the tissues of the leaf begin to grow a round ball-like structure enclosing the young insect. Eventually this sphere may grow to be an inch or more in diameter. The thick walls of the gall itself are rich in food upon which the insect feeds, and at the same time the tissues of the gall are filled with bitter tannin which

92

These spherical galls on oak leaves contain larval wasps. The galls furnish both food and shelter for the young wasps.

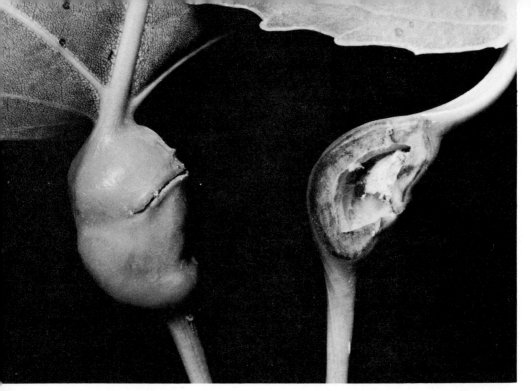

These galls on cottonwood leaf stems are produced by aphids. When the aphids are ready to leave, the lips of the gall open and liberate them. The gall at the right has been cut open to show the cavity.

make it distasteful to most other creatures. The young wasp is thus provided with a safe home and supplied with abundant food. In time the larval wasp becomes full grown and then changes into the adult or winged wasp, which emerges and flies away to make galls on other leaves.

Another gall-making insect is a close relative of common aphids or plant lice. In this case the gall is an enlargement on the leaf stems, or petioles, of cottonwood leaves. In spring the leaf stem begins to enlarge as a result of the aphid's presence until by early summer it has reached the size of a marble. This gall is hollow and inside there develops a colony of aphids. Now by a remarkable example of timing, a slit appears across the side of the gall. This slit appears just when the aphids are ready to emerge as winged individuals. If the slit were to open too soon, enemies might enter the aphids' snug home and

94

destroy them, but the gall-forming mechanism, whatever it is, works in such a way that the timing is perfect and the slit opens just when the aphids are ready to leave. Of course, we should remember that these gall-making insects are actually injurious to the plants they infest. Some of them, in fact, do serious injury to the plants upon which they are formed.

Each gall-making insect produces its own characteristic gall, even when it is on a different plant or leaf. Thus, the insect inhabitant may be identified merely by the kind of gall it has produced.

These galls are of almost every shape that one can imagine; they vary from the spherical shape of the "bullet" galls to the strange "flower" galls resembling flowers. They occur on almost all kinds of leaves from sagebrushes to oaks. Those found on oaks are perhaps the most common, but you can find them almost anywhere. Many galls are produced on leaves, either

These leaf galls on sumac were also formed by aphids. Each gall is hollow and filled with hundreds of aphids or plant lice that find a happy home within the gall.

This strange growth on the underside of a hickory leaf was produced by an insect that lived inside.

on the blades or the leaf stems. Other gall-making insects form their galls on twigs or the stems of plants. You are probably already familiar with the common goldenrod galls. These are green swellings on the central stalks of goldenrod plants, and if you cut one open you will find a white grub inside. If left undisturbed, this grub will eventually develop into a pretty fly that will emerge from the gall the following spring.

In ancient times people knew about these strange growths, but they did not know what caused them. As a result, there were many superstitions concerning them. One kind of gall was used for the production of the best kind of non-fading ink until very recent years. There are galls that grow on scrub oaks near the Dead Sea that are known as "mad apples" and were once used as a source of turkey-red dye. Some of these galls contain considerable sugar, and, since they are quite nutritious, have been used as human food. One kind is often found for sale at fruit stands in Mexico City.

96

CHAPTER 9

The Leaves of Autumn

$\mathcal{A}$ll of us are aware that as summer draws to a close the leaves of most trees change color and eventually fall to the ground. All summer these leaves decorated the twigs with their graceful shapes, so it is with a certain degree of sadness that we see them leave the trees. We know, of course, that with the arrival of spring the trees will drape themselves again in green cloaks. This is some consolation; still we hate to see them go because this event marks the end of summer.

Some trees such as pines do not shed their foliage in autumn, so we call them *evergreens*, but those trees that lose their leaves each fall are said to be *deciduous*. Most of the trees growing in the temperate zone belong in this latter class and it includes the oaks, hickories, elms, maples, poplars, aspens and many others. The evergreens do shed their leaves, of course, but not all at once. If you have ever walked through a pine forest you have no doubt noticed that the earth was carpeted with a layer of dead pine needles. Pines keep their needle-like leaves for several years and then discard them. In the Tropics trees do not normally shed their leaves all at once except in some regions having distinct wet and dry seasons. Most tropical trees drop and replace their leaves one by one so that a person is never really conscious of the changing seasons.

The leaves of trees are like old clothes that are discarded

when they are worn out and no longer useful. A leaf, as we have previously seen, is primarily a food-manufacturing plant, so when it has accumulated an abundance of waste material and is tattered by wind and the feeding of insects, it is no longer of use to the tree. We usually think of trees as being the only plants that shed their leaves, but the truth is that many smaller plants also discard old and worn-out leaves. Some plants, for example, continually add new leaflets at the top or growing tip and drop the older leaves at the lower part of the stalk. The top leaves are always the youngest. This shedding and replacement goes on all summer.

But let's have a close look at tree leaves that fall. You may wonder—if you have ever thought about it—how a tree "knows" when it is time to cast aside its summer foliage. Most people think that it is merely a matter of the leaves being touched by frost and then falling. Actually, it is not that simple. Have you ever noticed that trees growing near street lights usually keep their leaves later in the fall than other trees? This is because the hours of daylight have been lengthened for them so they are more like the long days of mid-summer. There are actually several factors that cause a leaf to fall. We have seen how plant growth regulators or *auxins* caused a plant to grow toward the light. It has now been discovered that similar auxins also control the falling of leaves. A healthy leaf is continually producing these auxins and sending them down the leaf stem or petiole through tiny ducts. The presence of these auxins, in some way which is not fully understood, prevents the formation of a *separation layer* of cells across the leaf base. It is at this separation layer that the leaf breaks off the twig in autumn. This layer consists of a layer of thin-walled cells and is also called an *abscission layer,* a term that comes from a Latin word meaning to "cut off."

When the days grow short in late summer, or sometimes when severe drought occurs, these separation layers develop

98

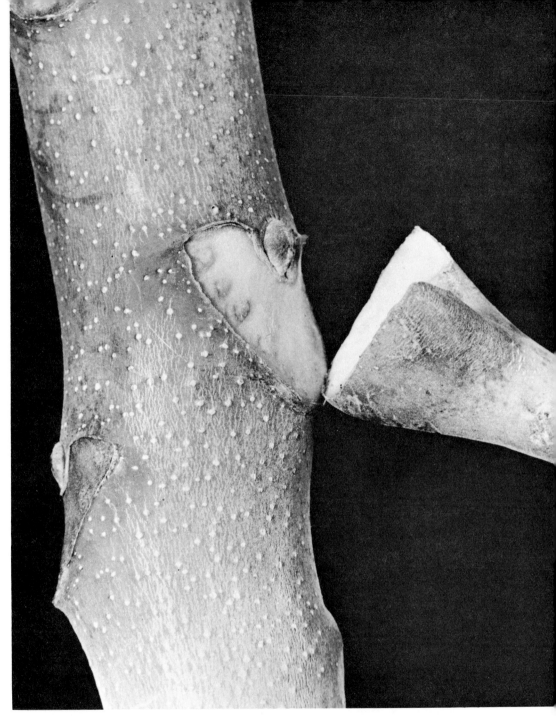

At the approach of autumn a "separation layer" of cells forms across the base of each tree leaf and the leaf then drops off. This close-up shows the base of a leaf in the process of breaking off of a twig, leaving a characteristic leaf scar.

across the base of each leaf stem and the leaves drop from the tree. A badly injured leaf will also drop. The specific process is not completely known, but it all has to do with the auxins that control the formation of the separation layers.

When the leaves have broken away and fallen from the twigs, small leaf scars are left, and these scars are more or less like fingerprints, just as leaves themselves are. Many trees can be identified in winter merely by identifying their characteristic leaf scars. Making sketches of the leaf scars of all the common trees in your vicinity would make an interesting winter nature project. Another fascinating study could be the way in which various tree leaves fall. Some leaves float down like tiny airplanes while other kinds spin as they drop to the earth.

The manner in which trees shed their leaves is interesting, but far more intriguing are the gorgeous colors with which Nature paints the forests each fall. It is like a grand finale to the pageant of summer. Those of us who live in the United States, England or Europe are apt to take autumn coloration as a matter of course, not realizing that this annual display is enjoyed by only a small proportion of the world's population. Autumn coloration occurs only in the temperate regions where grow the oaks, hickories, sumacs, maples, aspens, gums and other deciduous trees. In the United States this coloration is especially brilliant in the eastern half of the country.

Autumn colors range through almost the entire range of the spectrum and include red, scarlet, orange, yellow, and sometimes even bluish or purple tones. These latter colors, while unusual, are sometimes seen in persimmon leaves. Each kind of tree usually dresses itself in its own characteristic hue, but, of course, there are exceptions. Differences in soils and soil acidity sometimes influence the pigmentation of the leaves. Gold or yellow is the favorite color of black locust, hickory, tulip poplar, catalpa, quaking aspen, sycamore and birch. Brilliant red colors are found in the sumacs, some oaks, maples, sweet gums,

A cottonwood leaf scar

A hickory leaf scar

When leaves fall from the twigs in autumn small scars are left which are called "leaf scars." These scars are more or less like fingerprints, since each kind of leaf leaves its own special kind of scar.

dogwoods and sourwoods. One of the most colorful of all is the sumac, but nothing surpasses a sugar maple in its full autumn dress of scarlet. The maple is more spectacular than the sumac because of its larger size.

We may enjoy the autumn style show of the trees without knowing where they get their varied hues, but the colors will be appreciated even more if we understand how complex is their origin. When an artist paints a picture, he uses paints containing various kinds of pigments or coloring materials. By mixing these in various proportions he achieves the desired result in the finished picture. In a way, this is how Nature, too, paints the trees of autumn. Her pigments, however, are applied in an entirely different way. As we shall see, some of the colors are already in the "picture"; we just don't see them.

You will recall how the leaf manufactures starches with the aid of chlorophyll or green coloring matter. This green chlorophyll is actually present in leaves in the form of tiny capsules. These minute capsules look green, and they actually *are* green, and float in the sap within the leaf cells. Now inside these chlorophyll capsules there are also tiny globules of two plant pigments caled *carotenoids*. One of these is *xanthophyll* (pronounced zanth-o-fill) and the other is called *carotene* (pronounced care-o-teen). It is believed that these two pigments help the chlorophyll in some fashion in its work of food manufacture during the summer while the leaf is actually working. These two pigments are colored. Xanthophyll is yellow, while carotene is orange or red. They are present in such small amounts, however, that their color during summer is hidden by the bright green of the chlorophyll.

When summer comes to a close and short cool days arrive, the living processes of the leaf begin to slow down, and the chlorophyll that was so important to the leaf when it was busy making starch, begins to disappear. There is nothing then to hide the colored grains of xanthophyll and carotene and the

102

leaf looks yellow or red, depending upon the shade of the pigments. It is thus that Nature "paints" the poplars, birches and many other trees. The above pigments are very common in leaves; that is the reason that yellow and orange are the most familiar autumn tints.

But you may ask, "Where do the bright scarlet and red colors of sumacs and maples come from?" Leaves receive these colors from the presence of another class of pigments called *anthocyanins* (pronounced an-tho-cy-a-nins). These pigments come in assorted colors ranging from scarlet and red to purple and blue. During summer they are not present in the leaf but are formed during autumn. Anthocyanins also give many flowers their gay colors, and the common beet its blood-red tint. Unlike the first pigments mentioned, the anthocyanins are not confined to capsules but are water-soluble or capable of being dissolved in water. They appear chiefly in the upper cell layer of the leaf and thus often mask the color of the other pigments deeper down within the leaf.

Due to this combination of the various pigments in the leaf layers, the leaves often exhibit unusual colors. For example, if the reddish carotenoids deep within the leaf show through an upper layer of bluish anthocyanin the leaf looks brilliant crimson. Various tree leaves show all sorts of amazing colors due to the various combinations of these pigments. Some leaves even show a purple tint at times, a color produced when blue anthocyanin is present in the upper cell layer while green chlorophyll is still present deeper down.

There is still another substance that is sometimes present in leaves and affects their color. This is *tannin,* a bitter substance that causes green persimmons to taste puckery. Actually, tannins are waste products that impart brown colors to some autumn leaves. They are abundant in oaks, hickories and walnuts.

We now come to the question that most people are interested in. What kind of weather conditions favor the tinting of autumn leaves? The answer to this question is not simple, yet there are some factors that can definitely be said to bring about the rich colors.

We have already seen that the deep green color of chlorophyll masks or hides the colored granules of yellow or yellowish caretenoid pigments (xanthophyll and carotene) during the summer. When the days grow short, the leaves begin slowing down their work and the chlorophyll gradually disappears, allowing the yellowish carotenoid pigments to show. This accounts for part of the leaf color. Remember that at the approach of autumn a separation layer of cells begins forming at the base of each leaf. This separation layer tends to cut off the movement of sugars down the stem. Each leaf thus becomes isolated from the rest of the tree, and the sugars tend to accumulate in the leaf tissues. This favors the formation of anthocyanins. Anthocyanins, as you will recall, are very colorful pigments, ranging from bright red to purple. Thus, the leaf changes from summer green to all sorts of shades, from light yellow to deep red or even purple, depending upon the presence of the different pigments. Sometimes we see a "blush" of color in some leaves in spring which is caused by the formation of anthocyanins early in the season.

Autumn weather conditions have a direct effect upon the coloration of leaves, as everyone knows. It is obvious that a sudden hard freeze simply kills the leaves before their color develops, and they merely turn brown and fall. When this occurs there is little autumn color.

The most favorable temperatures for leaf coloration are cool, but not freezing, nights. Dry weather conditions tend to favor the formation of anthocyanins since it speeds up the changing of leaf starch into sugar. The most brilliant colors, of course, appear when conditions are favorable for anthocyanin formation within the leaves. Such conditions consist of dry summers followed by early autumn rains which prevent leaves from falling

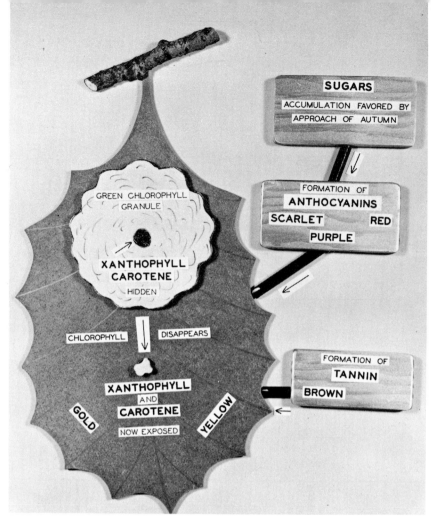

This model shows how the leaf "dye factory" works in autumn. During summer the green chlorophyll granules hide the granules of xanthophyll and carotene. At summer's end the green chlorophyll disappears, exposing the yellow and golden hues of xanthophyll and carotene. The approach of autumn also favors the accumulation of sugars in many tree leaves. This, in turn, favors the production of anthocyanins which dye the leaves various shades of scarlet, red, or even purple. Some leaves contain large amounts of tannin, giving them a brown color. These various methods of producing colors are found in many combinations.

too soon. For maximum color the autumn nights should be cold but not cold enough to kill the leaves suddenly. On the other hand, wet weather in late autumn results in dull leaf coloration. Thus does Nature paint the hills with all the gorgeous colors of the rainbow for the annual pageant of autumn.

These are leaves of the ginkgo tree. Scientists consider these trees to be "living fossils" because most of them became extinct during the Ice Age. Only a few living in China survived. They have been recently introduced to many other countries.

CHAPTER 10

Leaves of the Past

S ometimes we are apt to think that the world as we know it today has always been the same. The fact is that the world and its plants and animals are always changing. These changes go on so slowly that we cannot tell the difference from year to year, or even from century to century. Time moves very slowly in nature. For example, the time since the days of ancient Egypt seems very long to us, yet there are actually many trees still living today that sprouted while the pyramids were being built. Still, when millions of years pass, changes in plants do occur.

If we turn back the clock of time far enough we find that plants and their leaves have certainly changed. If we turn the clock back far enough, we come to a time when there were no plants at all. That was so long ago that it is lost in the dim mists of time.

Scientists who probe into the history of the plants of the very distant past are called *paleo-botanists* (pronounced pale-e-o-botanists) and these people have learned a great deal about the plants that once clothed the earth. Most of what they have learned has been obtained from the study of *fossils*. These, as you may know, are the petrified remains of plants—and animals—that once lived. If you have ever looked into a quiet woodland pool, you have probably seen dead leaves that had settled down to the bottom of the sand and mud. If these leaves were to remain in the pool for a long while they would, in turn, become covered with mud, and year by year be buried deeper and deeper. Now suppose a million years were to pass. By that time the leaves would probably have become turned into stone by the slow seeping of minerals into the leaf tissues so that perhaps even their microscopic structure would be preserved. This is how fossils are formed, and it is from these fossil remains that scientists learn about the plant life of past ages. It is often surprising how much detail can be seen in these leaf fossils. Each vein is preserved in stone just as if it had fallen from the tree only yesterday. There are even fossil fruits, flowers and other plant parts that give us additional information about ancient plants. Believe it or not, scientists even find fossil pollen grains from flowers long dead. As a matter of fact, the study of fossil pollen is so important to geologists that they have given it a special name, *palynology* (pronounced pale-e-nol-o-ji).

There is still another way in which leaves or leaf fragments have often been preserved. The trees of long ago sometimes exuded resin or gum that ran down their trunks. If a small leaf became imbedded in this resin, it was preserved in the transparent gum which slowly hardened into a plastic-like substance called *amber*. Leaves and insects so preserved show just as much detail as they did in life countless ages ago.

Fossil leaves are found in many places and in many kinds of stones that were formed from the slowly hardening sediments of ancient rivers and lakes. Some fossil leaves were also preserved when the falling ash from erupting volcanoes buried them. Sometimes you can actually find these interesting plant and animal fossils in exposed banks of streams where the water has washed away the soil. Other places to look are cuts where highways have been built through hills. Perhaps a local geologist can tell you the best places to search.

It is by means of these fossil plants and leaves that scientists

108

piece together the past history of plant life. It is a fascinating study that requires great patience and a thorough knowledge of botany. Reading the story of plant ancestry in the rocks is very difficult. It is something like trying to piece together the events in a novel that has had all its pages torn apart and scattered over an acre of ground. Still, by the careful study of fossils, and other bits of geological evidence, scientists have been able to put together the pieces of the puzzle and to learn how our present day plants were slowly developed from ancient kinds.

It will help us, perhaps, to appreciate the wonderful world of plant life if we do know something about the long road the trees and plants have followed before they became what they are today.

Geologists divide the earth's past history up into a number of *eras* and *periods* which mark the transitions between characteristic ages. If we go back about half a billion years we come to the time when there were no land plants at all. The only plants in the world were *algae* that floated in the ancient seas. In these seas, too, there were fishes and other aquatic

Many millions of years ago the only plants were algae or thread-like water plants resembling the ones shown here greatly enlarged. The dark bodies inside the algae are chlorophyll granules which manufacture its food.

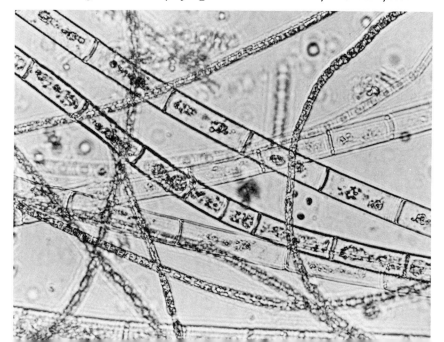

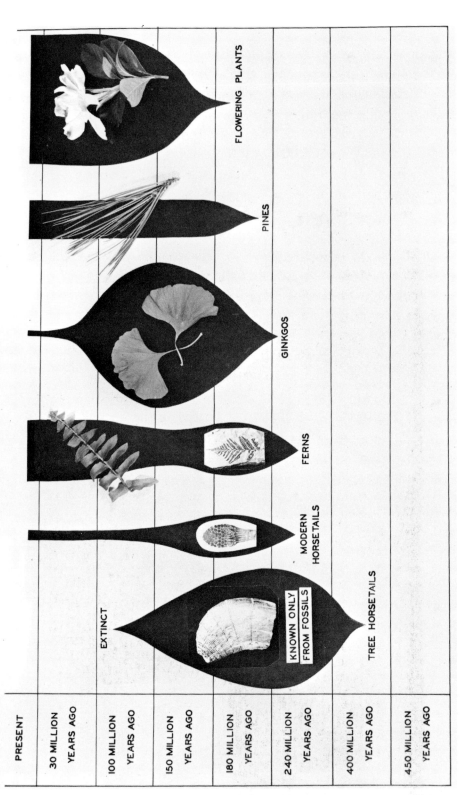

This chart will help you to understand how the various plants came into existence in past geological ages. The widths of the black areas indicate abundance of the plants as the ages passed. The tree horsetails became dominant and then disappeared over a hundred million years ago. All the other types are still growing today. We are now living in the golden age of the flowering plants.

creatures, but the land was barren, what there was of it. There were no mountains in North America except the Appalachians where active volcanoes spewed forth hot lava, and the Arctic seas rolled across what is now Canada.

Then, slowly the continent emerged from the sea, and a large section of the country from what is now Michigan to New York became a desert. As the ages slowly crept past, some continents of the world arose above the sea, and others settled. Mountains pushed thousands of feet into the sky and then slowly sank again as if in slow-motion. The land seemed restless and never satisfied to remain as it was. Fossil sea shells can now be found on the tops of the highest mountains, and the remains of marsh-loving plants occur in dreary deserts where only sand drifts in the wind today. There is evidence that the earth has passed through many alternating periods of quiet and intense activity. For a few million years the continents would be rocked by volcanic activity and then there were long periods of calm during which plants and animals thrived. We are living in one of these calm periods today amidst a veritable world garden of trees and flowering plants. As you may know, many thousands of years ago the last, or most recent, ice age began. At that time great sheets of ice began creeping down from the polar regions. This ice layer was perhaps a mile thick and very heavy. As it crept southward it ground rock against rock and gouged out valleys. One can still see the marks it left on the rocky walls of many valleys where it left its "signature" in the form of deep scratches. Eventually, it covered all of the area of Canada and part of what is now the United States and Europe. Those plants that could not stand the frosty temperatures were killed. The hickories in both Europe and Asia disappeared, and the giant Sequoias which once spread all the way across the United States retreated to small areas of California where they still live today. Ginkgo trees, which had once been common almost everywhere, were destroyed except for a few survivors that escaped the cold and were later found in China where temple priests had preserved them.

As the thick ice sheet pushed slowly southward the climate below it became cooler, and plants and trees that once lived only in the Canadian regions now began to grow in southern climes that had grown cold in the breath of the ice mass. Spruce and fir trees began growing in southern Florida far from their native habitats in northern United States and Canada. Paleobotanists have learned this from fossil leaves of these trees found in Florida and other southern states.

Then, slowly the Ice Age came to a close, and the vast sheet of ice slowly melted. As its edges retreated northward, plants and trees that preferred cool temperatures followed until northern United States and Canada as well as Europe became forested again. But we still have some of the Ice Age left. The entire central portion of Greenland is still buried under thousands of feet of glacial ice. Yet, geologists know that figs, magnolia and camphor trees once grew there. Strangely, up until a few years ago, it was evident that all of the glaciers of the world were melting. Now, however, it has been found that they are beginning to advance again! Does this mean that another ice age is already beginning? Only time will tell.

Most scientists, however, believe that we are now about two-thirds of the way through the last inter-glacial era, or period between ice ages, and that another ice age will not come for 10,000 to 15,000 years. There is nothing new about these ice ages. They have been creeping down from the polar regions now and then ever since the first plants appeared. No one knows what causes them. Perhaps they occur when the earth begins receiving less heat from the sun.

Let us now go back to the time of the primitive plants and see how they have slowly changed into the kinds found today. We will begin our story in Devonian times, a name for a period which takes us back nearly four hundred million years. The

This is a portion of a fossil tree horsetail that lived 200,-000,000 years ago. These tree-like plants had no limbs, and their "foliage" was more like twigs than leaves.

This graceful fern leaf grew many millions of years ago. Somehow it became buried in mud and slowly turned to stone as the surrounding mud hardened. It is now a fossil.

only plants that grew then were quite simple. Their leaves were small or they had none at all. They included the club-mosses and horsetails which still live today. They are marsh-loving plants, so we assume that the ancient lands where they grew were marshy. As time passed, larger kinds of plants entered the scene. A few of them were tree-like and resembled ferns.

At the close of the Devonian period there was a great increase in the world's dry land. It is believed that a great land mass appeared that extended from South America across the south Atlantic to include Africa and on to include what is now the Indian Ocean and Australia. Another great land mass extended across the Northern Hemisphere. This, of course, enabled land plants to extend their ranges for a long way so that the ancestors of many modern plants were found all the way around the world.

This brings us to the most exciting age of all from the point of view of plants, the one that geologists call the *Carboniferous* age. It began about three hundred and fifty million years ago. The climate of the world at that time was very warm and in many places there were wet marshy conditions in which plant life flourished. Probably the landscape looked somewhat like the great Okefenokee Swamp in Georgia does today, except that the "trees" were far different from those with which we are familiar. There were no flowering trees or shrubs and no flat leaves like those on modern plants. The trees looked like large horsetails, and their leaves were scale-like or long and narrow. A few were fern-like. It was near the end of this age that the ancestors of the modern pines appeared. It was during the Carboniferous age, this time of luxuriant plant growth, that the coal beds were laid down. The steamy atmosphere and sub-tropical heat were favorable to the development of great peat bogs which often accumulated to a depth of many feet. This was brought about by the slow accumulation of dead plant

114

The stem of this modern horsetail is about the size of a pencil, but millions of years ago its ancestors grew to the size of trees. Its leaves are small and scale-like. The horsetails belong to an ancient family of plants.

material which was later covered by sediment and then slowly turned to hard coal.

At the end of this coal-forming or Carboniferous age the earth went through another of its periodic changes. Thus dawned the *Permian* age which began about two hundred million years ago. Slowly the great coal-forming swamps disappeared, and much of the earth's surface became desert-like. Some kinds of plants disappeared, and others changed. The tree-like horsetails began to decline but the modern horsetails were just beginning. There were ferns similar to modern kinds. This was the time, too, when many other modern plant types began their histories. The tree-ferns, or *cycads*, also began to flourish and would do so for many millions of years until their decline in recent times. The same was true of the maidenhair trees or ginkgos. This was the time, also, when the great family of modern pines began their expansion on the world scene and their increase in importance until the present. Many other trees, too, appeared and left their fossil leaves in the rocks. But there were no flowering plants or trees yet. These were still millions of years in the future.

The world scene now shifts to the *Mesozoic* age, which began about a hundred and eighty million years ago. Gone are the great club-mosses and horsetails with their unbranched trunks. Instead, there are trees with spreading branches like modern kinds. Ginkgos and tree-ferns still flourished, but there are also at long last, flowering plants that resemble magnolias and buttercups. In spite of this, however, there are still few plants with modern-looking leaves. Along with the rise of the vast tribe of flowering plants there appeared trees of infinite variety that lived and died and scattered their leaves like calling cards in the sediments of ancient rivers and lakes.

Sequoia trees thrived all the way across the world from Europe through Siberia and on to Greenland. Cypress trees, too, were almost world-wide in range and left fossils of their needle-like leaves in stones. The range of the walnuts was far greater than it is today, and their leaves were quite similar to those we see now. There were actually more different kinds of poplars than in modern times. The oaks, too, are an ancient race that had its beginnings in the dim past, and it is probable that the remote ancestors of the squirrels gathered acorns in the pre-historic forests of oak. As time passed many of the trees that had once grown everywhere in the world were destroyed over most of their ranges by the Ice Ages, leaving survivors in isolated places. This was true of the magnolias, ginkgos and sequoias.

From that point on, the story of the world's plant life is one of slow change. Those plants that could not adapt themselves to changing conditions passed out of the picture and were replaced by more vigorous kinds. As the great ice sheets advanced down from the pole, arctic blasts more terrible than any known today swept the land again and again. But the earth's plant life flourished in spite of everything the climates of the past could do to it.

Today delicate flowers bloom upon the hills and in the valleys, and each spring the trees unfurl their fresh green leaves to the sun. But back beyond each leaf there are a billion years of history, a history written in the wonder of living leaves and recorded in fossil stone.

Exposed shaley rocks such as these along the margins of streams and lakes often contain fossil plants. These rocks were formed when the ancient sediments of rivers and lakes hardened into stone. Fossils may often be exposed by separating the layers of stone.

Key to leaf identification chart on page 14

1. Weeping willow
2. Cottonwood
3. Hackberry
4. White oak
5. Sumac
6. Maple
7. Sycamore
8. Ginkgo
9. Honey locust
10. Pine
11. Red buckeye
12. Sassafrass
13. Sweet gum
14. Elm
15. Mimosa
16. Tulip poplar
17. Red cedar
18. Redbud
19. Dewberry
20. Holly
21. Black oak
22. Nandina
23. Post oak
24. Fig
25. White ash
26. Catalpa
27. Bald cypress
28. Hawthorn
29. Magnolia
30. Silver maple
31. Hickory

Index

Page numbers in italics are those on which illustrations appear.

119

About the Author

Entomologist Ross Hutchins is also an expert photographer, and this combination of interests has resulted in almost thirty years of studying, photographing and writing about insects, plants, animals and birds. Born in Montana, he grew up on a cattle ranch near Yellowstone Park. At Montana State College he majored in biological sciences and later he took his Ph.D. in zoology and entomology from Iowa State College.

Dr. Hutchins' articles and pictures of natural history subjects have appeared in encyclopedias, books and magazines, among them *National Geographic, Life* and *Natural History,* and European publications such as *Sie und Er, La Vie des Bêtes* and *Sciences et Avenir.* A special interest in unusual insect and plant life led to his own books in the juvenile field—INSECT BUILDERS AND CRAFTSMEN; INSECTS—HUNTERS AND TRAPPERS; STRANGE PLANTS AND THEIR WAYS; and WILD WAYS.

Ross Hutchins now lives in Mississippi where he is Entomologist and Executive Officer of the Mississippi State Plant Board and head of the Department of Zoology and Entomology at Mississippi State University.